Awaken Your Inner Genie

Discover Your Power, Heal Your Life, Change the World

Paola Knecht

Knecht Publishing

Knecht Publishing

Cover illustration and design: David Colón

Proofreading and comprehensive editing: Julián Chappa

For the souls that seek, at last, to be set free.

Contents

Disclaimer

This book details the personal experiences and opinions of the author regarding mental and physical health, but neither the author nor this book are a substitute for your trusted physician.

We want to make it clear that this book can never serve as a substitute for consultation with a licensed healthcare professional, such as your trusted physician. Before starting any health program or making any lifestyle changes, you must consult your doctor (or another qualified healthcare professional) to ensure that you are in good health and that the examples contained in this book will provide significant benefits.

This volume provides content related to physical and/or mental health issues. As such, its use implies your acceptance, as a reader, of this "Disclaimer."

Introduction

When I was a little girl, one of my favorite stories was *Aladdin and the Wonderful Lamp*, one of the tales from *One Thousand and One Nights*. I was captivated not only because it allowed me to imagine the spectacular mystical Persian landscapes of that era, but also because of the magic and mystery surrounding the magical lamp.

Who hasn't dreamed at some point of stumbling upon a magical lamp that, with a simple rub, would release a genie capable of granting all our wishes? It's likely still the dream of most people. We love the idea of being rescued by someone: a savior, a God, a genie, a politician, a leader... or our parents. We cling to the belief that there's something or someone out there who will save us from this murky world, from our problems, and ultimately, from ourselves.

How wonderful and convenient it would be to have a genie inside a lamp who could fulfill all our desires!

Would you believe me if I told you that such a genie does exist, that it spends most of its life asleep, but if you call upon it, it appears?

What's behind that mystical tale we heard as children, which was painted as a fantasy that doesn't align with how our "reality" works? For many years, I thought something like that was impossible, that a genie who could fulfill all my dreams was nothing more than a product of movies and fantastical stories that had nothing to do with reality.

Our reality, as I learned from childhood, is something that exists on its own, fixed, uncontrollable, dangerous, where you have very little influence over the events that unfold. I learned to see reality as something that happened without my ability to prevent it (and much less to understand it).

My role was simply to stay alert to what was happening and react. When something bad happened to me, I told myself that "God willed it so," that "Things happen for a reason," and my only option was to resign myself because "That's just how life is." That capricious life that no one understands. That last phrase reminds me of a popular song from my university days, by the Mexican rock/pop band Elefante, which went something like this:

"That's how life is, so capricious,
Sometimes dark, sometimes rosy pink,
That's how life is, so flamboyant,
It takes, it gives, it lifts you up and brings you down, and sometimes it gives you what you want..."

In short, we see ourselves as puppets carried by the wind, and it seems our only option is to try to come out unscathed from life's twists and turns. It's no surprise that most people feel this way. From the moment we're born, our minds are programmed to fit into a society that exists precisely because of this collective conviction that things must be as we're taught to perceive them.

When we're newborns, we don't know the concept of "reality," nor do we understand the classification of things. We don't comprehend that time exists, nor that we must adapt to certain limits and norms that we learn as we grow. As we mature, we learn that to coexist with other human beings, we must perceive the world and its forms in the same way as our society does as a whole.

If, for some reason, you don't fit into that model of a human being as part of the social construct, then you're definitely "weird." In our childhood, if you're a rebel who doesn't pay attention in class or disobeys your parents, you're immediately labeled as someone with ADHD (Attention Deficit Hyperactivity Disorder), which is defined as a "disorder," read here as something "abnormal," like an illness, typically affecting children and even diagnosed into adulthood.

The symptoms are difficulty paying attention, problems controlling impulsive behaviors, and hyperactivity. According to experts on the subject, one of the negative consequences of this disorder is classified as "serious problems," which for children means poor grades and for adults can even lead to job loss, among many other issues.

Basically, if you're not a docile and obedient person, you represent a problem for society (or perhaps for those who control societies and disguise themselves as leaders). Of course... they fear the genie coming out of the lamp to wreak havoc...

Through this book, I invite you to reflect on the true consequences of awakening the genie in the lamp. That genie is your consciousness, your true Self. The lamp is the confines, metaphorically speaking, of the mind and body.

When we manage to free the genie that lives within us, we will experience the true consciousness of the universe and realize that we are co-creators of reality. In other words, it's possible to conceive our dreams, and there is no limit to what human consciousness can achieve.

Throughout the chapters of this book, you will learn to:

- Awaken the genie within you, harnessing it to work in your favor to fulfill your deepest desires.
- Transcend the limits of what we consider "reality" and tap into dimensions where so-called "miracles" can occur.
- Heal your relationship with your inner genie, which will allow you to heal your personal relationships.
- Transform your world as a systemic result of having healed your inner genie and,

> consequently, the relationships around you, which affects the "whole" of your reality.

In the first part of the book, we will begin with an inner journey to understand how our genie was captured at the moment of birth and how it has remained asleep until we decide to awaken it through our consciousness.

In the second part, we will explore how to free your inner genie by healing your relationship with yourself. This healing has transformative power, allowing you to notice a change in your personal relationships. Gradually, these relationships become less conflict-ridden; you stop attracting negative and toxic energies and make room for energies aligned with those emanating from your true consciousness. You'll realize that you can develop good and better relationships with family, friends, and the people around you.

In the third part, we will see how this change will be reflected in your reality. You'll have a new perception of the world, which will be shaped according to the nature of your consciousness, the co-creator genie that has designed that reality as you perceive it from your true genie nature.

I promise you that, after embarking on this journey together, you'll never again look at the story of Aladdin with skepticism!

Part One

Awakening The Inner Genie

Chapter 1

Trapped in the Magical Lamp

"As with many things, what matters is not what is outside but what is inside."
—Aladdin

To begin our journey, we must first understand how we became trapped in a "magical lamp." Of course, I'm using the "magical lamp" as a metaphor to describe our mind, our body, and the reality within which we operate. How did this imprisonment of our own soul begin? Have we ever truly been free?

This is not an easy question to answer. In fact, this question may have been debated since the beginning of time. In the Christian religion, it's said that it all started when the first humans to walk the Earth, Adam and Eve, disobeyed God by eating the forbidden apple, manipulated by a serpent that convinced them to consume that fruit.

From that moment on, we were labeled as "rebels." In this story, Eve (the woman, the feminine, creative energy) succumbs to the temptation of the serpent (a symbol of intelligence, betrayal, and deceit), who persuades her to eat from the tree of forbidden fruit, which would also grant them knowledge. Eve then convinces Adam to eat it as well. When God discovers what they've done, He condemns them to a planet where they must suffer to earn their place, as cited in Genesis 3:

"God said to the woman: I will greatly increase your pains in childbearing; with pain you will give birth to children. Your desire will be for your husband, and he will rule over you.

Then God said to the man: Because you listened to your wife and ate from the tree I forbade you, the ground is cursed because of you. Through painful toil you will eat food from it all the days of your life. It will produce thorns and thistles for you, and you will eat the plants of the field. By the sweat of your brow you will eat your food until you return to the ground, since from it you were taken; for dust you are and to dust you will return."

Coming from a "good God," these words sound like a cruel condemnation for humanity. What fault do we, the descendants of Adam and Eve, have for their disobedience to their God? Why didn't God want Adam and Eve to eat from the fruit of knowledge? Is the message of Genesis that we should have remained servile and ignorant to deserve Eden, but because we rebelled, we deserve to suffer and live in perpetual suffering?

The truth is that much of humanity lives exactly like this: imprisoned in the spell of suffering. Slaves to their inevitable fate. They live in fear of being judged by a superior God who sees everything, judges them, and punishes them for being "disobedient."

Though I was raised with the teachings of the Catholic religion, I refuse to believe that God harbors such a resentful energy. In any case, I find the teachings of Buddhism, the fourth largest religion in the world, founded in India about 600 years before the birth of Christ, far more acceptable.

Buddhism is based on the teachings of a prince named Siddhartha Gautama, who attained enlightenment at the age of 35 after meditating for 49 days under the Bodhi tree. Siddhartha teaches that our greatest prison is our attachment to suffering and dissatisfaction.

According to Siddhartha (or Buddha), humanity's problem is that we don't realize the world as we perceive it is an illusion, and clinging to this illusion as we perceive it causes deep dissatisfaction and anxiety.

That's why most of humanity, trapped in this illusion, desperately searches for a way out, that ultimate state of happiness, peace, and tranquility. The problem is that we often look for these things in the wrong places. We believe that having more money—or a bigger house, a new trip, or a better job—will lead us to that ultimate state of peace.

Of course, we later realize that achieving what we desired is only the beginning of a series of more and more desires, and fulfilling them doesn't lead to ultimate happiness but to an endless abyss of desires until, at some point, we collapse. As the iconic song "Afuera" by the Mexican rock band Caifanes says: *"And you think you can believe, and have all the power, and suddenly, you have nothing."*

Once we realize we're in this illusion-prison, the process of true awakening begins. Believe me, very few people in the world have come to this realization—you're likely one of those few. That's why you're interested in this book and understand what I'm talking about. In my social circle, most people still haven't realized that we live in an illusory prison. They go through life simply worrying about carrying out their daily activities.

From a very young age, I had the impression—or intuition—that there was something more than what my eyes could see. Even when I dreamed, I was certain I had actually been to those exotic places, that what happened in my dreams was truly happening somewhere in this vast existence.

I couldn't conceive that only what I experienced in my "waking hours" was all that existed. Moreover, much of what I observed in this world seemed illogical to me. I still remember walking in nature with my father, watching the birds fly, the ducks swim calmly without a care in the world, and one day I asked him:

—"Why are animals smarter than us?" My father looked at me, confused.

—"Why do you think they're smarter?" he asked.

—"Yes, animals are smarter because they don't have to

work or follow rules to live. They're just there, enjoying their existence without having to pay for anything or ask for permission," I replied.

—"You're a perfect fit for the nickname 'La Roca Foucal,'" my father responded, letting out a nervous laugh.

—"What does that mean?" I asked, looking at him puzzled.

—"It's the nickname for people who think a lot," he concluded.

Since as a child I had more pressing concerns—like waiting for the next episode of my favorite show or counting down to three in the afternoon to go play with my friends—I didn't bother to find out what "La Roca Foucal" meant.

My father passed away when I was only eleven, and those childhood conversations I cherished in my mind were tucked away in the trunk of memories. Many years later, on a train ride to work, I read in a book about the maxims of the French philosopher François VI, Duc de La Rochefoucauld. Just reading the name instantly transported me back to my childhood and my talks with my father.

There I was, sitting on a train on my way to work in the Zug region of Switzerland, thousands of kilometers away and more than 25 years later, when that sensation of living timelessly in a parallel life resurfaced. I finally learned that "La Roca Foucal"—read "La Rochefoucauld" —was a French writer, aristocrat, politician, soldier, poet, and philosopher, famous for his *Maxims* (Reflections or Moral Sentences and Maxims), a collection of brief, sarcastic aphorisms about human nature, society, and morality.

His *Maxims* were written in a somewhat cynical tone, demonstrating that humans act based on self-interest, where vanity and hypocrisy reign and are the root of complexities in human relationships.

I still haven't found the connection between La Rochefoucauld's writings and the innocent (perhaps ignorant?) questions of my childhood. Maybe my father saw something in me—my rebellious spirit, my sarcastic questions—or maybe the comparison itself was, in the end, a joke. I don't know, but these little incidents in life hold great meaning for me.

Who would have thought that years later I would actually become a writer addressing philosophical topics like the nature of reality and consciousness? That's why I believe that time doesn't follow a linear path but a quantum one.

I recalled this story because it was the first time I realized that asking these simple, perhaps innocent, questions is how you begin to call your genie out of the lamp.

Questioning What You See Is the Beginning of Freedom

The higher a person's level of consciousness, the greater

their freedom. Questioning reality as we see it is what opens the door to a higher level of consciousness.

One of the ways we remain prisoners of our own existence is by accepting circumstances "as they are" without questioning whether what we believe we see makes sense. That's the secret that the power elites hide so zealously from the masses to prevent us from rebelling and letting our genie out of the lamp.

Among the many books that discuss the desires of an elite to control the population, one that particularly catches my attention is *The Protocols of the Elders of Zion* (henceforth *Protocols*). I had heard about the existence of this book for some time, but recently I came across an interview with former Dutch businessman Ronald Bernard, in which he publicly revealed the existence of a financial elite he was once part of, which, according to his account, bases its financial practices on the teachings of this work.

It's a text published in 1902, originating from Tsarist Russia. Considered antisemitic and propagandistic, it details the plans of a "Jewish conspiracy" aiming to dominate Freemasonry and control communist movements in all nations of the world, with the ultimate goal of total global domination.

It's said that these protocols are the result of various secret meetings held at the First Zionist Congress in Basel, Switzerland, in 1897, presided over by Theodor Herzl, a Hungarian-born Jewish journalist, writer, and playwright, founder of modern political Zionism and officially known as "the spiritual father of the Jewish state."

What strikes me about these protocols is that, despite being labeled as false and a clear attempt at disinformation by "conspiracy theorists," the degree of similarity between how modern society functions and what the Zionist members of that society were allegedly planning to dominate humanity seems to be unfolding with striking precision in these modern times.

For example, the *Protocols* declare that freedom is merely an idea, that people with bad instincts outnumber those with good intentions, and that, because of this, it's relatively easy to govern through violence and terror. If we turn on the television at any time of day, the first thing we see is the number of conflicts and wars unfolding somewhere in the world.

I tested this by turning on the TV to see what the narrative of the day was. As I write these lines, the war between Russia and Ukraine continues; Israel plans to intensify attacks against the Palestinian people; China is encircling Taiwan's borders; tensions are rising between Iran and Israel; the U.S. elections are causing deep polarization in that society... Without a doubt, what reigns in the world right now is chaos and violence.

The true purpose of so-called "liberal" governments is to take advantage of human weakness to seize power. In the past, power was imposed directly and brutally through wars and invasions. Today, that same blind and brutal power hides beneath what we call laws.

Laws are a highly effective tool for keeping societies subdued "within a legal framework," a set of decrees that, upon closer examination, are simply a collection of ideas promoting liberalism, which ultimately consists of sacrificing the true gift we have as humanity: freedom.

I mention all this because, even if the *Protocols* were false, when you study them closely, they reveal with astonishing precision how societies are being manipulated by current governments. What back then was merely a series of ideas and principles for "dominating the masses" is now, in the 21st century, essentially the construct of our modern societies.

Awakening our inner genie doesn't mean obsessing over verifying whether the *Protocols*—or any similar document—are true based on what experts (or the media) tell us. Our task is to study them, question them, observe reality, and start asking questions. Tyranny is based on the idea that human nature is corrupt, craves power, and is therefore capable of sacrificing the well-being of others to maintain its apparent power.

Personally, I believe that while human nature has its corrupt side, it also has its luminous side. And if the corrupt side dominates our societies, it's because it's the dominant power in the world at the time of our birth.

We grow up in an environment where societies are already trying to impose the rules of the status quo on us. As we grow, we mold ourselves to all those external forces that dominate societies. We learn to follow the rules of the game to achieve "success" in life, in a life governed by Luciferianism.

We spend the precious time of childhood locked within four walls, learning standardized things (school time), to be shaped into a little soldier defending the system. Then you must work and contribute to the oppressive machine with a job that, in the best of cases, is irrelevant to your personal growth.

And to ensure you don't rebel, they fill you with meaningless distractions like social media, the internet, television, shallow celebrities, and banal entertainment. This way, they ensure you have no time for personal growth or reflection. They also ensure that the genie never comes out of the lamp or, worse, that you believe freedom means staying trapped inside the lamp.

Freeing Yourself from Mental Confinement

To free yourself from the suffering that comes with identifying with external circumstances, you must elevate your consciousness. A low level of consciousness manifests as constant dissatisfaction.

For the liberation of consciousness—what I call true human progress—we must set a goal that allows us to unite two worlds: our inner world (our true identity) with the outer world we see (reaching our true destiny), to materialize what we have truly come to do in this world.

The current social system has normalized victimhood

as a common human behavior; even groups aspiring to power benefit from this victim mentality to achieve total manipulation of the masses, in exchange for false promises that ultimately vanish into thin air.

Our family tree can also be an obstacle to recognizing our true selves. Families tend to impose false goals on us, which we consciously or unconsciously adopt as our own.

For example, when you decide to study medicine because your father was a doctor, or from a young age, your mother enrolled you in ballet classes and pressured you to spend your few free hours after school in exhausting training and rehearsals.

Perhaps to please our parents or grandparents, we submit to their desires, their unfulfilled goals, and they pressure us to be the best at it to "bring honor to the family." Their goals are projected onto us, and our true desires sink into the depths of the subconscious.

However, there comes a moment when those frustrated desires surface and cause great suffering through physical and psychological symptoms (chronic physical discomfort, addictions, relational conflicts, somatizations, feelings of anxiety, depression, etc.). Then we must ask ourselves: What is this symptom or feeling trying to tell us? What is it that you truly want to say that you haven't said, or do that you haven't done?

This is why people who have achieved "success" as defined by their parents, partner, or immediate social circle often end up depressed, lost in addictions, or even take their own lives after supposedly "reaching the top."

Liberation begins when you awaken to a level of consciousness where you realize that identifying with the classifications and trivialities of the world causes you suffering.

"MIRACLES HAPPEN BY OPERATING AT A HIGHER LEVEL OF CONSCIOUSNESS. THEN DESIRES BEGIN TO COME TRUE."

Chapter 2

How Miracles Work

"Miracles occur naturally as expressions of love."

—A Course In Miracles

Another one of my favorite childhood movies was *The NeverEnding Story*.* The plot goes something like this (sorry for the spoiler!): The kingdom of Fantasia was in danger because its Empress was mortally ill. People no longer believed in Fantasia. The salvation of the kingdom depended on a warrior named Atreyu, who had to find the Empress and save the realm. In the end, the only way to save Fantasia, as the Empress explained, was for a human child—in this case,

* The NeverEnding Story is a fantasy film released in 1984, based on the novel of the same name by German writer Michael Ende. In some Latin American countries, it is also known as The Story Without End.

Bastian, who was reading the story as it unfolded—to recognize that the kingdom of Fantasia truly existed.

When Bastian realized that he held the power to save the kingdom of Fantasia, he could hardly believe it. How could an ordinary child like him be capable of saving even the great warrior Atreyu, the Empress, and the entire kingdom? How was it possible that he could determine their fate simply by reading a book?

The more Bastian doubted, the more the kingdom crumbled, facing the real danger of falling into darkness, into nothingness. The Empress watched with great sadness as Fantasia faced imminent destruction, and then she shouted to Bastian with all her might:

"You can save us! You just have to believe!"

"I believe! I believe!" Bastian finally shouted with all the strength in his lungs, and the kingdom was saved.

"You just have to believe!"

That phrase stuck with me and pierced my heart. What does it mean to believe in something? How can believing in something save an entire kingdom? You might wonder why I've chosen this story to start a chapter about miracles. In my view, this story metaphorically represents how miracles work.

Perhaps we should start at the beginning. What is a miracle? According to the dictionary, a miracle is "an event not explicable by natural laws and attributed to supernatural intervention of divine origin." Miracles are often interpreted as something rare, extraordinary, marvelous, or even impossible.

From the moment we become aware of the world, we're instilled with the perception that life is a series of events over which we have no control, whether things go well or badly for us. From a very young age, we're taught to fear life through the fear of death. Life is a fragile event, a miracle in itself. What are the odds of staying alive day after day?

We grow up with the idea of an unpredictable world, to some extent violent and dangerous. As a general rule, our life is simply about surviving. All the events that occur in our daily lives revolve around this idea of staying alive. We take for granted that difficulties, bad luck, illness, crises—all these are part of everyday life.

When something good happens to us, we see it as "a stroke of luck," something fleeting that surely won't happen again. We assume that our daily life only includes challenges, dramas, scarcity, and dealing with all kinds of fears. What if I get sick? What if I lose my job? What if I have an accident?

It's precisely when something breaks this pattern of negative thinking that a miracle emerges: that stroke of luck, that "unthinkable" event we attribute to chance. We believe miracles are like that rare impossibility we're fortunate enough to experience once in a while.

Otherwise, miracles are only possible in science fiction movies. And let's not even talk about who can make miracles happen. Only saints, witches, and shamans. Performing miracles is something unavailable to the average human. At least, that's what we've been led to believe.

At the same time, many of us believe in God. Some see God as an omnipotent, supreme being watching us from the heavens, judging our actions. Others interpret God as an energy, a source that transcends all classification and form.

Regardless of how you see God, one thing we believe is that God protects us, enlightens us, and shows us the way. In Christianity, we believe that Jesus is the human representation of God on Earth, who came to share teachings about what a human being is capable of doing.

Jesus Christ worked through miracles. He healed the sick, made food appear where there was scarcity, turned water into wine. He transformed the lives and hearts of those who met him. He was a loving, beautiful, and perfect being—a holy person. The holiness he taught was nothing more than the pattern of thought and action that God designed for humanity. Being like Jesus is like following God's original design.

Of course, churches, religion, and doctrine distorted the true intention and turned it into a tool to generate fear and control the masses. Religion preaches that miracles can only be performed by beings superior to humans, such as demigods or gods. Something a common, sinful human could never dream of becoming. Our only option is to accept our sinful nature, be subservient, and repent for our sins.

It's within this belief system, largely spread by religion but also by other political, educational, and social institutions, that we distance ourselves from miracles and perceive them as something we can only dream of but will rarely access. In my humble opinion, this is far from the truth.

Miracles Happen Every Day

In my personal view, miracles happen every day and at every moment. The issue is that we've become so accustomed to them that they no longer seem like miracles. We consider them ordinary, something we take for granted, without recognizing their divine nature. I can give you a list of miracles that happen every day without you paying much attention to them:

- The simple act of waking up alive each morning.
- The sun rising every morning to give its light and warmth, sustaining life on Earth.
- Pure water.
- Nature, alive and expressing its most marvelous form at all times.
- The love you feel for your closest loved ones.

- The way thought emanates from consciousness.
- The body's ability to heal itself.
- The creativity that leads you to do extraordinary things.
- The smile of an innocent child.
- How radiant flowers, plants, and trees grow from tiny seeds.
- The birth of a human being.
- The functioning of the brain.
- The breeze on a warm summer day.
- Majestic mountains.
- The marvelous landscapes of nature.
- Classical music.
- Fruits born from the earth.
- The universe.
- The stars.
- The first gaze of a newborn baby.
- The sea.

I could go on listing everyday miracles, events that people have normalized as "ordinary." Everyone takes for granted that the sun will rise each morning and that, at dusk, the moon and its stream of stars will come to adorn the sky.

Many of us don't have to worry about whether tomorrow morning, upon waking, we'll have enough food or shelter. Nor do we worry about whether we'll breathe or not (our body does it automatically without us noticing), or whether we'll have enough water to drink...

All of that is already a gift and a miracle. If we paused for a moment from the frenzy of our daily lives and observed life more closely, we'd realize that miracles are the norm, the natural—not the exception.

Human beings are capable of performing miracles every day; it's even part of our co-creative nature. The problem is that we don't believe we're capable of manifesting them, let alone deserving them. That's why, before discovering that we're capable and worthy of miracles, we must first believe it's possible.

Miracles are simply expressions of love. To realize your ability to perform and receive miracles, you must first heal your relationship with your inner self. This is what I call "healing" and ultimately "freeing" your inner genie. That genie, once freed, is capable of granting your wishes —it only needs to escape the confinement of the lamp.

It's your relationship with yourself that prevents you from seeing that you're capable of performing miracles and that you yourself are a miracle. That's why forgiveness is the natural expression of love, and love is the creative energy of miracles.

The Perception of Miracles

Every form of life on Earth has an energetic function. Josep María Fericgla*, a Spanish writer and anthropolo-

---

* Spanish writer and anthropologist, with a degree in History and a doctorate in Social Anthropology. He focuses on the study of shamanism,

gist, mentions in his works that our function as humanity is to create consciousness.

All forms of life have some degree of consciousness. From minerals, which operate with a very basic, almost imperceptible consciousness—their atoms and molecular structures communicate with one another and can change their biochemical composition when altered. Plants absorb these minerals and use them as nutrients through their roots to develop.

Plants have a basic consciousness that fulfills their energetic function on Earth. Animals have a higher degree of consciousness than plants: they are aware of their bodies and even develop affectionate feelings.

Humans are the only beings on Earth capable of developing consciousness of their own consciousness. In other words, our consciousness goes beyond the body. Of course, our primary consciousness is tied to the body's needs—for example, we worry about clothing, food, staying warm, satisfying emotional and sexual needs, etc. But we're also conscious of what we think.

HOMO SAPIENS ARE THE ONLY SPECIES ON THE PLANET THAT QUESTIONS THOUGHT ITSELF: "WHY DO I THINK WHAT I THINK?"

---

expanded states of consciousness, and the use of entheogens in various cultures around the world. He presides over a foundation that bears his name: www.josepmfericgla.org/.

The ultimate degree of human consciousness is transcending the body and realizing that consciousness doesn't create the body, but rather consciousness creates the body. As Jacobo Grinberg-Zylberbaum states in his Syntergic Theory, "consciousness, not matter, is the foundation of reality. What we call matter is a manifestation of consciousness."

Consciousness is the state that induces action, though it doesn't inspire it. In other words, you're free to believe whatever you want, and your actions bear witness to what you believe.

Another way to recognize that we've reached a higher degree of consciousness is when we begin to feel the presence of the "silent witness." That witness who observes everything but remains on the sidelines. That observer belongs to the realm beyond the body and sensations.

When we learn to meditate at a level where we can observe thoughts "from the outside," we experience the sensation that someone is watching us.

That mysterious, omnipresent being who sees everything and encompasses everything. It's precisely that Being who is capable of manifesting miracles, because they come from It. The body is merely the receiver capable of manifesting the miracle. That "silent witness" is your Higher Self. The Self that extends beyond the common perception you have of yourself. It's the expanded reality of the Self.

And so, you create the sunrises. You create the sea breeze. You create the events that happen during the day.

The feelings that emanate from the Being are created by the Being. You respond to what you perceive, and as you perceive it, so you behave.

If you awaken to this reality, you'll realize that miracles can only come from within yourself. Miracles occur in a mind prepared for them. It's a unified, coherent mind that operates in the light. It's free of fears, lacks, and doubts. A mind with absolute certainty of the existence of light.

The unified Being realizes that it contains everything. The external world is nothing more than the reflection of an expanded Self. That's precisely why it's popularly said that your personal relationships are like a mirror: in those relationships (good or bad), you can discover a part of your Being.

I confess that, on a personal level, it took me a long time to accept that my personal relationships were a reflection of my own way of being. Before, if I had to deal with someone I didn't like, I felt a knot in my stomach.

When I worked at a large company, I recall a time when I had to give a presentation to a group of leaders. In this group, there were some I got along with well and others I preferred to avoid. When I had to speak with one of the ones I didn't like, I'd think, "Oh no, now I have to deal with this annoying person. They have such a huge ego and only believe what they think and say is right." So, when I had to face them, I'd approach the interaction with that discomfort already ingrained in me, and our interactions would feel awkward.

One day, I meditated on that person in particular and decided to conduct an experiment. First, I began to change my perception of them. I told myself, "This person is just a human being who surely has fears, worries, and only wants to feel approval, to feel that their existence matters. Isn't that the same thing I want and feel?"

Then I asked myself, "How would I like this person to treat me? How would I like our relationship to be if I could choose?" And so, I began to imagine us greeting each other cordially, listening to one another, and ultimately collaborating in a more synergistic way.

In my subsequent meetings with this person, I mentally prepared myself in the most positive way possible. I imagined we'd have a cordial, pleasant, and constructive conversation. I won't say it happened immediately, but it did happen faster than I expected. When I changed my perception of this person, something magical happened. I noticed a change in their tone of voice, in the way they spoke, and I even sensed they relaxed more when we talked. We even shared a couple of laughs on some occasions. I listened more attentively and developed more empathy. I realized that, ultimately, we were seeking the same goals, but each of us was trapped in our own ego.

By changing my perception of that person, the way I treated them changed, and consequently, the way they treated me transformed as well. For me, this is a simple but very clear example of an everyday miracle. The miracle, in my view, lies in the ability to transform energy in a positive and unifying way. This process operates independently of time and space. That's why, in some cases, miracles are perceived as "instantaneous." Sometimes we perceive that they take more time, but most often, transformations in energy happen imperceptibly.

For example, changing my perception might produce an instantaneous change in the source of energy and what I project toward my colleague, but it's not something obvious or perceptible. Only after some time do you observe the transformation. Isn't this how we perceive all natural processes, like watching a flower grow or how a small layer of snow can form massive avalanches?

When we plant a seed, from our perspective, it seems like nothing changes on the surface until some time passes, and you start to see the first sprouts. That doesn't mean there's no activity beneath the surface—it's just that we lack the ability to perceive it from our perspective.

In the end, I came to the conclusion that we create miracles ourselves from our subconscious, that miracles are governed by the same fundamental principles as Creation itself. Therefore, miracles are expressions of love and unification; they represent the truth.

"THE ONLY WAY TO UNDERSTAND THIS SUPERPOWER WE HAVE TO CO-CREATE MIRACLES IS THROUGH FORGIVENESS."

Forgiveness is the key to accessing true peace. In the following chapters, we'll explore what true forgiveness toward oneself means and how that forgiveness will help you heal your relationships—not only with yourself on all levels: emotional, intellectual, material, and creative. By healing yourself, you'll heal your personal relationships and, as a logical consequence, automatically contribute to the healing of the world.

Part Two

Healing The Relationship With The Inner Genie

"Every man, even in tragic conditions, can decide who he wants to be—spiritually and mentally—and preserve his human dignity."
—Viktor Frankl

The relationship we have with ourselves is the hardest one to heal. Our entire lives, we've been subjected to the expectations of an external world that, most of the time, demands too much of us.

Our schools didn't offer courses on how to get to know ourselves. From the moment we entered primary education, we were imposed a curriculum that had nothing to do with our personal interests or spiritual development. All that mattered was learning mathematics, natural sciences, history, geography... subjects that, I don't deny, are fascinating if we could choose which specific topics to explore.

The reality is that traditional education has been one of society's most effective tools for disconnecting us from our true Self. From a very young age, we're forced to follow strict school schedules, complete assignments, obey authority, and learn to live in a community. That left little time for reflection, observation, free play—in other words, for the key activities that allow us to develop our own thinking.

Then, as we grow up, we're bombarded with all kinds of social expectations. You have to study a career, get a job, get married, start a family, buy a house, follow the same steps as everyone else. If you don't, you're a failure, a social misfit, a slacker. You're not "contributing" anything of value to society.

Especially in the Western world, the worship of productivity and material accumulation has become an indicator of a person's success or failure. Are you unemployed? You're a loser. Are you "just" a housewife? Surely you're a lazy freeloader who doesn't want to work. Do you want to spend your day simply reading and meditating? What a waste of time—you're not making money that way!

In a society obsessed with consumerism, productivity, and measuring results through material possessions or the accumulation of "experiences" to show off on social media, there's no time to even stop and think:

Who are you?

WHAT HAVE YOU COME TO DO IN THIS WORLD?
IS YOUR MISSION SIMPLY TO WORK IN ORDER TO CONSUME?
TO CONSUME IN ORDER TO LIVE?

My friend, it wouldn't surprise me if you feel lost. Above all, because your entire life you've learned to live disconnected from your true Being. In his book *Breaking the Habit of Being Yourself*, Joe Dispenza mentions that we're only superficially aware of our Being. You might think that when you make decisions in the world, you do so fully consciously. For example, you wake up in the morning, take a shower, have your first coffee, get ready for work, etc. You believe you're doing all of this completely consciously, right?

The reality is that only 5% of the mind is conscious; the remaining 95% is governed by the subconscious[*], made up of a series of "programs" we've automated over time.

Let's recall the famous experiment by Russian scientist Ivan Pavlov on classical conditioning. One day, Pavlov noticed that dogs salivated whenever they saw food. He wanted to know if this was an automatic conditioning or if it could be modified. Later, he decided to ring a bell before

* Timothy D. Wilson (2002) *Strangers to ourselves: Discovering the adaptive unconscious*. Cambridge, MA: Belknap Press of Harvard University Press.

feeding the dogs. So, the dogs would hear the bell and know that food was coming.

Over time, Pavlov observed that just hearing the bell caused the dogs to salivate, even if no food was in sight. The same thing happens with our subconscious mind. By repeating the same actions and associating them with specific feelings or bodily sensations, the body records them as "consciousness" and can reproduce them "unconsciously."

If we compare this to our daily lives, you'd be surprised to see how many things you do during the day have become habits. Routine activities that you always do the same way. Not only the actions—even your emotional reactions to those activities are the same each time.

Think about a feeling you closely identify with and ask yourself why you feel that way. What actions or thoughts make you relive that feeling over and over again? On a personal level, I admit that I was trapped by the feeling of guilt. Having been raised in a traditional environment, I pressured myself to meet all the social expectations heaped upon me.

I wanted to always be the best student, the best daughter, the best friend to everyone. I wanted everyone to think I was a good person. And every time I made a mistake, I felt guilty, as if everything was my fault for not being good enough at everything.

Over time, I got used to that feeling of guilt, and it even became comforting. It turned into a "comfort zone." If I made a mistake, if I did poorly on an exam, or if a romantic relationship ended, I simply blamed myself for everything. I was the poor fool who wasn't capable. I'd get depressed, write in my journal, and after a while, I'd feel better... until another incident happened. Then I'd activate my feeling of guilt again. I'd tell myself, "This is happening because you're foolish, naive, because..." (and a long list of etceteras).

It's hard to break free from that addiction to negative feelings because they're so deeply ingrained in our subconscious programming that sometimes we don't consciously notice when they're triggered. That's why, if we want to feel differently, we have to think differently.

To Feel Differently, We Have to Think Differently

This is where our real effort lies if we want to change. To achieve total self-acceptance, we must deprogram the mental software we've been feeding our entire lives. It sounds easy, but it's a task that requires time, seriousness, and above all, a fierce determination to want to change.

In deep healing, positive thoughts alone aren't enough. It's also necessary to teach the body to change the biochemistry that comes with thinking differently. That's why simply declaring "I want to be happy" or making an intellectual decision like "Starting tomorrow, I'll only have positive thoughts" won't work. It won't work because, while your conscious and intellectual mind reasons that it wants to be happy, your body has been trained for years to feel negative emotions.

I don't know if this has happened to you, but I know exactly what it means because I've lived it myself. I've tried declaring, "From now on, I'm only going to be happy," but deep down, I knew something wasn't right. No matter how much my intellect thought I wanted to be happy, my body was so accustomed to negativity—for so many years and through so many means—that, naturally, at the first exposure to reality, I'd feel unhappy again.

Changing negative programming isn't simple, which is why we must develop compassion for ourselves. We have to understand the magnitude of the enemy we're dealing with.

We're talking about programming that has been feeding your mind and soul since the moment you were born. A baby, when born, only knows the love for its mother. It's a pure, natural love, biologically necessary for survival. The baby intuitively knows that without the mother, its life is in danger. That's why it cries when it's first taken from the womb.

The second feeling we learn is fear. Fear of dying, of not having food, of not having love, of danger... And that's the crux of the matter, because most people—from a very young age—are conditioned to live in fear. Fear of loss, of disobedience, of suffering, of illness, of loneliness... of all kinds of conditioning.

Our parents tell us that if we don't finish our plate of food, we'll be punished. Teachers tell us that if we don't do our homework or behave badly in class, we'll get bad grades. The news tells us the world is dangerous: wars here and there, financial crises, protests here and there. The danger of global warming, the danger of pandemics, the danger of pollution... danger, danger, and more danger!

And then, you have to fear society's expectations. Fear of not having a job, fear of not finding a partner, of not being able to start a family... or fear of having to start a family. Fear of not making money, fear of losing money. Fear of not finding the right partner. Fear that people will think you're a loser... fear, fear, and more fear!

It's no surprise that our body is accustomed to unhappiness. It's easier to generate negative feelings than positive ones. Negative feelings are so deeply rooted in us after so many years that they've become an automatic process. That's why it's important to realize how our thoughts, even the ones we consider most insignificant, are shaping our reality at every moment.

Our body memorizes and associates thoughts with emotions instantly. The memorization of emotions works like this: when we think something, it evokes a memory. That memory triggers an emotion. Notice what you feel when you recall something tragic in your life.

There's a saying that goes, "To remember is to relive." When you recall an event, you likely also evoke what it made you feel. If you remember a loved one who has passed away or the loss of your favorite pet, you'll probably feel bad.

A THOUGHT THAT CREATES AN EMOTION, OVER TIME, BECOMES A MEMORIZED EMOTION.

To deprogram past feelings that cause us pain, we must elevate our consciousness to a level that allows us to observe the mechanism of thought without being emotionally affected. Emotional detachment from memories is a difficult task to achieve, but not impossible. All it requires, in reality, is neutralizing the emotion through forgiveness.

I keep insisting that forgiveness is a powerful tool for inner healing. Forgiveness acts as a catalyst because it neutralizes memorized feelings. Forgiving yourself is, in a way, freeing yourself from a heavy burden of stones you didn't have to carry in the first place.

Personally, I believe forgiveness is a form of unconditional love, necessary for healing our self-concept. As psychologist Walter Riso says in his book *Fall in Love with Yourself*, "Most of us carry an invisible stick with which we beat ourselves every time we veer off course or fail to meet our personal goals."

One way to forgive ourselves is to make a conscious effort to change our perspective of ourselves. To be kinder about the concept we have of ourselves, to recognize that making mistakes is part of the human condition and that, at times, we make wrong decisions. But that doesn't mean we have to punish ourselves so harshly.

Forgiving is replacing attack with acceptance. Forgiving ourselves is recognizing that the light of truth lies in accepting ourselves as we are. Healing the relationship with ourselves is, in a way, admitting the reality of who we are. Attacks against ourselves stem from the belief that we're not worthy of happiness.

Do you believe the world you live in is chaotic, tragic, full of misery and pain? The world is, in part, a reflection of our inner self. We've chosen to accept that the world is this way; we've let ourselves be manipulated by what we're made to believe. It's time to make peace with yourself.

The world is a reflection of your mental peace. If you feel you live in a world where everything is misery and pain, it's because you identify with those concepts. I know it's hard to accept that we have a responsibility in perpetuating human misery.

You might ask: How is that possible if all I want is to live in peace? How can we live in peace if we accept negative thoughts as true? Something doesn't add up.

WE CANNOT ASK FOR AN HARMONIOUS WORLD WHEN WE OURSELVES DON'T FEEL HARMONY.

We cannot ask the world to love and respect us if we don't first love and respect ourselves. The world is a mirror, a reflection of our consciousness. That's why, if we want a better world, we must start by loving ourselves. We must heal that relationship with our Self, with our inner genie.

It's time to make peace and step out of the lamp for good. For that to happen, you must make peace with your Being. Your Being has many dimensions and operates at different levels of consciousness. In this world, your Being is an emotional Being, an intellectual Being, a material Being, and a creative Being. The totality of those Beings forms what you perceive as "the Self."

In the coming chapters, we'll explore how to heal each of those Selves.

> *"It's not about stifling the desire that exists in the heart of man, but about freeing it so it can reach its true height."*
>
> —Joseph Ratzinger

Chapter 3

The Emotional Being: Loving

This part of your Being is related to emotional energy, to the heart. It is your emotional genie. To heal the relationship with yourself, above all else, it's essential to learn to love yourself.

One of the first emotions we develop from a young age is the feeling of rejection, of anxiety about our existence. We feel threatened by "the world out there." We feel vulnerable, unable to see anything positive in ourselves.

That's why attacks from the outside hurt us. The yelling from our parents or the mistreatment from others toward us creates trauma that stays with you throughout your life if you don't let it go. Those wounds remain open, and when we reach adolescence and adulthood, we spend our lives hiding those wounds.

I firmly believe that depression and feelings of resentment, anxiety, and abandonment stem from those wounds stored in the unconscious part of our Being, often manifesting in destructive behaviors. Who is the first person you try to destroy? Yourself!

Feelings of destruction come from those unresolved childhood wounds, and the first person we blame is ourselves. You end up generating a sense of repulsion toward yourself for having lived those experiences, even if you were merely the victim of the attack. That's why it's essential to forgive ourselves before forgiving anyone else.

Forgiveness as a Healing Tool

The act of forgiving yourself is the most powerful tool for healing your emotional Being, your wounded emotional genie. It's also one of the hardest things to do as human beings. It's true that our families and society in general can be very harsh in their judgments, but the power of forgiveness lies solely within you.

FORGIVING YOURSELF IS THE FIRST STEP TO HEALING THIS WORLD.

In essence, you create your world. The quality of your thoughts and emotions shapes the reality you live in, so the first transformative energy of the Being lies in the ability to love yourself. If you love and accept yourself, your perception of the world will automatically change.

You might now be wondering: How can I forgive myself if I can't forgive others? Excellent question! I know it's very difficult to forgive those who have hurt you, especially if it was a severe trauma like rape, physical and/or emotional violence, or abandonment by loved ones. Sometimes, it's incomprehensible for our wounded heart to imagine forgiving someone who has caused us so much pain.

The attachment to our physical and emotional Self is so strong that an attack on our Being feels 100% personal. In this dense world, it's completely understandable that forgiving someone who has hurt you is extremely difficult. However, it's essential to achieving true peace and fulfillment in our lives.

Detaching ourselves from the memory of the attack is, in fact, our salvation. Elevating our existence to a level of observation and detachment. Recognizing that the more energy you keep investing in recalling those past wounds, the more they flare up in your heart and the more they destroy you.

There's no room for negative feelings in love. We cannot truly love and, at the same time, harbor resentment toward ourselves or others. Before demanding to be loved, recognized, and desired, we can make a conscious decision, through personal effort, to recognize ourselves first. We can free ourselves from all those judgments made against us.

For love to flourish within us, we must honor that vital energy that keeps us alive. You have a mission to fulfill, so you must recognize that your existence itself has immeasurable value. You are part of Creation, of the Whole.

Your Being deserves all the love and respect in the

world because you are a reflection of the world, the beauty that emanates from existence. You are the architect of your reality, and you have an unimaginable influence on the lives of those around you.

That's why forgiveness is, ultimately, a liberation. It's the acceptance of a greater reality than the one we perceive in our physical world. For our Being to experience a new world where peace, harmony, and fulfillment reign in our hearts, we must forgive the old world. Forgive the old visions, that perception of separation. Our old perception of "having arrived in this world alone."

Forgiving is making room in your mind and heart for thoughts filled with love and positivity, forgetting the rest. It's a conscious decision to forget what we once perceived as a personal attack.

Feelings of revenge and resentment harbor negative and destructive energy within themselves. By continuing to feed them, we give them more attention and, therefore, more power. The hatred and resentment we feel toward those who have hurt us perpetuate the vision of being victims, of being a small being without the power to change their reality.

Accumulating and carrying all those negative energies only perpetuates a cruel world dominated by dark energies. Forgiving is making the deliberate decision to ignore those negative forces and not let them influence your life. When you finally remove the dark veil from your eyes to see the true light, it's *liberating*.

Generosity Is a State of Grace

When you are generous, it's because you've transcended the ghosts of negativity. Someone who gives with an open heart has overcome the fear of being hurt or unreciprocated. Those fears lose the foundation of their existence. Why should I fear if I have everything, because I can give everything?

Generous people aren't afraid to give because they know that the greatest satisfaction comes from feeling useful to others. Most people feel happy when they know they've helped someone become a better person. In a very intimate part of our Being, we are all connected to that feeling of unity.

Now, I'm not saying that "giving everything" means giving away your house, your car, and all your possessions to others and leaving yourself with nothing. In fact, I believe that would have a counterproductive effect on the true meaning of "giving." To be able to give to others, you must first be at peace with yourself. In other words, you must give to yourself before trying to give something to others.

YOU CANNOT GIVE WHAT YOU DON'T HAVE.

If you've traveled by plane, you surely remember the mini first-aid courses we receive before takeoff. The flight attendants instruct us that in an emergency, the first person who should put on a life vest and oxygen mask is yourself, before trying to help someone else, even before helping a child.

And it makes sense: without oxygen, how can you help someone more vulnerable than you? That's why generosity always comes from abundance—in thought, deed, and word. Positive thoughts of abundance generate spiritual and material abundance. Those who have abundance can always give and, therefore, be generous.

The problem with our current society is that most people live in a state of scarcity consciousness. They think that if they give, they're depriving themselves. If I give you a piece of my cake, I'm left with less cake to enjoy.

On one occasion, I interacted with a client who was terrified of giving too much, out of fear of "being taken advantage of." She felt that everyone wanted to exploit her, and as a result, her attitudes toward situations and people in her daily life were uncomfortable and tense.

What's interesting about this case is that with her own mindset of always suspecting others, she ended up attracting precisely those kinds of situations and people into her life. This reinforced her belief that "everyone wants to take advantage of her," creating a vicious cycle.

The only way out in these types of cases is to "break the spell." It sounds easy, but it involves deep personal work. It requires introspection to understand what makes you feel vulnerable about the act of giving. Often, the result is that you're unable to give because you feel incapable as a human being. You feel you're not good enough to contribute something to the world.

If I'm a "good-for-nothing," what do I have to offer? Therefore, being generous is an act of self-love. It's loving yourself enough. It's having healthy self-esteem that makes you feel complete. How can you be generous with yourself? Let's look at some illustrative examples:

• **Dedicate quality time to personal growth and reflection.** In this fast-paced world we live in, it's more important than ever to set aside personal time for introspection and connecting with your inner strength. Activities like reading a good book, meditating, walking in the forest, writing your thoughts on paper, listening to relaxing music, or taking a leisurely hot bath.

• **Practice self-forgiveness.** If you made a mistake or feel you failed at something important, close your eyes, take a deep breath, and forgive yourself for judging yourself so harshly. We are beings in constant evolution, and it's normal for things not to turn out as we expected sometimes. The important thing is not to be so harsh in judging yourself when you feel you've failed. A good suggestion for practicing self-forgiveness is to write yourself a letter acknowledging the mistakes made, while also committing to improving and reconnecting with your goals.

• **Take care of your body.** A visible act of love is treating your body with care and respect. Make an effort to provide it with quality food, respect its need for sleep, exercise it, and keep it in a state of relaxation as much as possible.

• **Maintain positive internal dialogue.** Positive thoughts not only benefit us by contributing to optimal mental health. Recent studies conducted by researchers at Yale and Miami* universities analyzed older adults for over twenty years and found that those who maintained a positive attitude during their aging process lived, on average, 7.5 years longer than those with a negative outlook. So, if you want to live longer, it's worth making a personal effort to maintain a positive mindset.

• **Allow yourself to rest and "do nothing."** Sometimes, the best way to reward yourself is to grant yourself moments of peace. It's giving yourself time to do nothing. Yes, exactly. Forget the daily demands and take a break from constant "doing." Did you know that doing nothing is a popular practice and even a legitimate technique? You may have heard of the *Niksen* method. It's a practice originating from the Netherlands that promotes precisely the "art of doing nothing." This practice, which became popular in minimalist social circles, involves dedicating moments of inactivity without a specific purpose, solely to let the mind rest and recover from daily stress. Some benefits associated with this practice include stress reduction, improved creativity, and a greater sense of overall well-being.

---

* Levy, B. R.; Slade, M. D.; Kunkel, S. R. & Kasl, S. V. (2002) «Longevity increased by positive self-perceptions of aging», en *Journal of Personality and Social Psychology*, 83(2), pp. 261-270.

Loving Yourself Is an Act of Faith

The act of having faith has multiple dimensions. In religious and spiritual contexts, having faith means having complete trust in a higher power. It could be God or a spiritual belief. From a more philosophical perspective, faith involves embracing mysticism. It's a way of facing life's mysteries with a positive outlook, an affirmation in the face of the unknown.

The act of faith involves trust. It's about having a positive conviction about what you believe in. That's why I consider loving yourself a true act of faith. It's accepting yourself unconditionally despite the uncertainty that your existence represents.

I don't know if you've ever found yourself wondering what you came to do in this world. Why do you exist? That question can cause a lot of uncertainty. How can I know what I came to this world for? Does my life have any meaning?

Perhaps the most crucial question we need to ask ourselves is, "What gives meaning to my life?" Then things can get very complicated. For someone who has had a difficult childhood or traumatic experiences throughout their life, answering this question might be especially challenging, particularly if they feel their life is filled with suffering.

Have we simply come to suffer? When you have faith in yourself, you know that your life goes far beyond the experiences you go through at specific moments. You know that your value as a human being cannot be measured because you are part of a magnificent Creation, infinitely greater than what's comprehensible.

Having certainty of this provides the foundation for healthy faith in yourself and in life. When a person has faith in themselves, they know that no matter what happens, there's always a solution. Painful experiences help us learn and grow, while beautiful experiences allow us to reaffirm our faith in life and in our Being.

Why is it important to have faith in yourself? I see faith as a compass. It's a guide for where to go when you feel lost. Imagine you're the captain of a ship at sea, with no idea where to steer your vessel. A compass helps you locate coordinates and indicates which direction to sail, depending on the course you want to take. Your faith acts as a compass and also as your lifeline.

You follow the compass with the conviction that doing so will lead you to your desired destination. Similarly, when you have faith in yourself, you respect your decisions and follow your path based on what you believe is the best you can do at each moment. You have faith in your decisions and, therefore, know you'll arrive at the right place.

In our society, less and less emphasis is placed on this important aspect of ourselves. The media, institutions, and other social organizations constantly try to manipulate us about what's right or wrong to do. They dictate how we should be and what we should like.

In the early days of the internet—especially toward the

late 1990s—we had a medium for self-expression, but soon the initial "democratization" became corrupted and, years later, turned into a monopolizing tool of what's now called "platform capitalism,"* which currently runs rampant.

In other words, at the beginning, social media democratized free expression, but today it no longer promotes authenticity. Instead, it encourages following others and comparing our lives to theirs, wanting to have the same things, which leads to various serious problems.

TO BE AUTHENTIC, ALL YOU HAVE TO DO IS CLOSE YOUR EYES AND LISTEN TO YOUR INNER GENIE.

Learning to Receive Is Also an Act of Love

Many people find it hard to believe that receiving is the same as giving. In fact, many people don't feel worthy of receiving. On one occasion, a client told me he didn't feel comfortable receiving a gift or a compliment because he felt pressured to "return the favor." He said, "When I receive something, I feel the pressure to give something back, and I don't have the resources to do so."

Giving and receiving are, in reality, the same act of love. It's a process of unification between two people, and it doesn't necessarily have to involve giving or receiving from the same person. You can give to someone and expect

* To delve deeper into the topic, I suggest reading the essay *Platform Capitalism* by Canadian writer and academic Nick Srnicek.

nothing in return, but rest assured that life will take care of unifying the action through another person or circumstance.

As writer and poet Maya Angelou expresses, "When you know, you teach. When you learn, you receive. Generosity lies in giving, but also in learning to receive." Giving and receiving come from the same source. When you give, you're opening the flow of abundance. You make way for generosity, and that same energy will continue to manifest in multiple, unimaginable ways.

Let's look at a specific example. When I was a student, a friend asked if she could stay at my apartment for a few days because she was going through a crisis with her partner. I agreed and even offered her food and lodging for free. At the time, as a student, I didn't have much money, so I couldn't support her financially, but I offered what little I had.

Days passed, and my friend found her own apartment and moved out. In the end, she stayed longer than agreed. She thanked me, said I'd done her a great favor, and promised to invite me to dinner one day to somehow repay the time she spent with me. I didn't give much importance to her promise, as my help came from the heart.

Life went on, and I didn't hear from her for a long time. One day, I had a family emergency and needed to return to Mexico. The problem was that I didn't have enough money for the plane ticket, and my family couldn't help me either. I mentioned it to another friend, and she managed to gather the money I needed through other colleagues who offered to support me.

I was amazed at how life works in this way. When I helped my friend in crisis, I didn't think about "charging her for the favor." I simply opened my home to her and offered everything I could within my means. Although she didn't directly repay the favor, in another circumstance, other people did me a huge favor that I truly needed at that particular moment.

I'm convinced that the act of giving and receiving is a unifying act, and since it comes from the same source, it's the same expression of love. As Alejandro Jodorowsky says:

> *"What you give, you give to yourself. What you don't give, you take away from yourself."*

There's still a false perception that when you give something, you're losing it. If you lend money to someone and they don't pay it back, you think you've "lost" that amount of money, and if that same person doesn't repay you, it means you'll never recover it.

Operating in that state of scarcity gives you the perception that there isn't enough for everyone, and that you have to cling to material and emotional attachments out of fear of losing them. There's no understanding of the true nature of reality: in this world, nothing goes to waste, and everything that exists is there for a specific purpose.

Everything that exists is there to serve you in one way or another.

Chapter 4

The Intellectual Being: Thinking

Our intellectual Being is our direct connection to the world we project as real. It is our intellect that helps us interpret life and the things around us. The intellect is directly related to the left hemisphere of the brain, which is responsible for logical reasoning, analysis, and language.

Having a good relationship with our intellect is a crucial element we must not neglect. Of course, intuition and the heart play an essential role in the totality of our Being, but our intellect is a fundamental part of that whole. If we aim to have a good relationship with ourselves, we must care for our intellect just as we care for our emotional Being.

At first glance, this might sound contradictory. Many trendy spiritual movements tell us that the intellect is actually of no use and that we should suppress our critical thoughts and let ourselves be guided by intuition. I agree that intuition can be more important than the intellect in many cases; however, I believe completely abandoning the intellect is a terrible idea.

My proposal is that we must respect, nurture, and cultivate our intellect. The better your relationship with your intellect, the greater your ability to develop strong intuition. I even believe that the two complement each other and don't repel one another, as is commonly thought.

Let me explain why this happens. To develop good intuition, you must somehow connect with a source of wisdom beyond the physical plane, one that guides you through sensory sensations—like the famous "butterflies in the stomach"—to indicate whether the decision you're about to make is right... or not.

If you rely solely on intuition without much knowledge of the matter at hand, the likelihood of making a mistake is quite high. On the other hand, if you have the necessary knowledge, develop critical thinking, and stay alert to the situation, when it comes time to make a decision, the knowledge you've acquired (combined with the sensory sensations the decision provokes) can provide a better indicator of whether what you've decided is good or bad for you.

Let's illustrate with an example. Suppose you have to decide between two job offers. Perhaps the first interviewer feels more likable than the second, which gives you a better "gut feeling" that the first job is the more suitable choice for you. But if you analyze other parameters more deeply—for example, the type of work, the tasks involved, the salary, the daily commute, etc.—you might realize that the second job is actually the better option, despite the "chemistry" with the second interviewer not being as strong as with the first.

If you had to make the decision based solely on intuition (biased by the positive feelings and empathy toward the first interviewer), you might miss out on the opportunity to choose the better job simply because you didn't do the intellectual work of evaluating both jobs impartially and rationally.

Language Shapes Your Reality

Thanks to language, we've been able to build entire civilizations, making it one of our most powerful tools for constructing realities. Through language, we can materialize thoughts, concepts, and ideas, serving as a bridge between creative energy and material energy.

In our three-dimensional world, everything begins with an idea. That idea, well-articulated, can become a material reality. This is how we transform ideas into matter.

Think about how buildings are constructed. Architects first have an idea of what the building should look like. How tall should it be? How many floors will it have? What will it be used for? How many windows will it have? What will the façade look like?

After imagining it, they begin to draw it on paper. In other words, they start creating the building's blueprint.

Then they deliberate on the materials, structure, finishes, and other details. The further the vision of the building progresses, the further its construction advances.

This is how our collective language has built the civilization we have today. Conceptually, language can be seen as a powerful algorithm of information, considering how humans structure, process, and transmit that information.

The language we use to communicate can carry creative or destructive energy, depending on the meaning we've assigned to the use of words. A language that conveys love, peace, and positive energy can transform an environment, filling it with harmony and peace. An aggressive, negative, and violent language can generate mental illnesses, depression, and anxiety.

It is our intellectual Being that is responsible for encoding information through language and writing, as well as decoding it when listening or reading the information in question. The interpretation in this process of encoding and decoding information is what gives meaning to words, concepts, and thoughts.

Ideas Are Transmitted Through Culture

Culture is a set of beliefs, values, and human behaviors shared by a community. Culture shapes how we perceive the world, so it's no surprise that the way we perceive reality is heavily influenced by the culture we were immersed in where we were born and raised.

The culture of your place of origin can determine religion, moral norms, arts, laws, and even the history and type of economy the group chooses to pursue. I was born and raised in Mexico, and from a young age, I was taught to follow the Catholic religion, the etiquette norms of Monterrey society at the time, and how I should "behave in society."

Back then, that family environment was my only truth. It was only when I had the opportunity to travel and learn about other countries and cultures that I realized my reality wasn't the only one that existed. Each group creates and shapes its own reality based on the cultural norms passed down from generation to generation.

What role does culture play in finding ourselves? Undoubtedly, culture can be seen as a "base programming." It's the first set of information we receive as children.

For example, a very traditional and closed culture can produce people who find it difficult to question reality or develop critical thinking. Conversely, in the context of an overly liberal and progressive culture, people may develop who constantly face identity crises and emotional instability because they grow up without any model or structure to follow.

As the popular saying goes, "All extremes are bad." It's important to know and acknowledge our culture, keeping in mind that we are heavily influenced by it in how we see (and interpret) life. In itself, this isn't a bad thing; however, it's also crucial to develop the ability to question, analyze, and reach your own conclusions about which aspects of your culture may be biasing you when making certain decisions.

Culture is your most intimate connection to the material plane. Your definition of yourself and what success means to you is—or can be—deeply influenced by shared beliefs about money, material possessions, and the social status defined by your group.

It's important to consider to what extent culture influences your thought process and, consequently, the way you make decisions. Making peace with your intellectual genie requires that the genie understands all the dimensions of its Being and to what extent its belief system is preconditioned by certain currents of thought.

How Religion Influences the Intellect

Religion has a decisive influence on how people live their reality. In fact, it's through religions that some of the most divisive ideologies in human history have been created.

As intellectual beings, our goal is to seek the truth. We want to find the meaning of our existence. We desire to unravel the mystery of life, and religion offers a refuge, a promise that there is an ultimate truth, providing comfort in the knowledge that we are not alone in the world.

Joseph Ratzinger tells us that "Man carries within himself a mysterious desire for God." In God, we seek to find that ultimate truth of existence. That which science cannot explain. Religions have encouraged humanity throughout history to develop a relationship with the mystery of life and have inspired us to create great architectural, literary, philosophical, artistic, legal, and ethical works as a way to materialize celestial beauty.

Religions seek to fill that void we can't quite satisfy. Humanity knows well what doesn't fully satisfy it, but it still can't imagine or define what would bring that absolute happiness, that nostalgia carried in the heart.

There are aspects of religion that have positively influenced us; among them, religion helps us deepen the search for meaning. It invites reflection on the meaning of life, to think about death and transcendence. As intellectual beings, we possess that curiosity and that unattainable sense of searching, which makes us question all the nuances of what we perceive as reality.

Practicing religion requires a certain mental discipline. Studying religious texts, meditation, and prayer foster concentration and contribute to developing critical thinking about oneself.

On the other hand, religion also carries certain negative aspects, such as dogmatism. A rigid or absolute religious practice can have the opposite effect: closing the door to an open mind and the questioning of new ideas and ways of seeing life.

Religion has also been used throughout time as a tool for control. Following the mandates of the Bible, the Quran, the Torah, etc., as if your entire life depended on it, has caused many people to live in fear of being "punished" by God, Allah, or the deity of the moment. Religious fanaticism, as we know, leads to war, violence, and destruction.

Therefore, I believe we must always remain vigilant not to fall into extremes with any ideology. Freeing the intellectual genie involves stimulating the intellect freely, openly, and without constraints, so it can reach its highest expression of genie.

Chapter 5

The Material Being: Living

Although our origin is cosmic, our level of consciousness in this world manifests in the material. The material Being is made up of all the things we perceive as that great sphere in which we live and express ourselves in the world.

The Body Is Your Sacred Temple

The body is the direct bridge that connects you to this world. It is like the temple where your soul resides while you live the experience of physically passing through this life. Your physical appearance is like a fingerprint you use to identify yourself in the world, which is why it feels like the closest thing to us.

In fact, most of humanity cannot distinguish their body from their existence. We know that the body without the soul is not existence; however, it is our bioenergetic conductor, the vehicle we need to enjoy the physical world. As our primary conductor, our body deserves the most sublime love and care.

By focusing on the struggles of existence, we forget to pay attention to our most immediate material possession. What good would it be to live surrounded by riches and splendor without a healthy body? In its original design, the body is an exquisite work of Creation, essentially perfect. It has the ability to self-regenerate and adapt to almost any external condition.

Although these days there's talk of Artificial Intelligence and even rumors of a possible replacement of people with machines, the reality is that we are still far from being able to develop something as complex and brilliant as the human mind and body.

Noam Chomsky*stated in a recent interview that Artificial Intelligence and language models are mere "software that commits plagiarism, because they don't create anything but copy the work of human artists, modifying it in a way that bypasses copyright laws."

Personally, I agree with Chomsky's opinion. While Artificial Intelligence can be a very powerful tool and help us perform tedious tasks more quickly and efficiently, in the end, it lacks the ability to create something new. That is something only the human mind can do in the material plane.

---

* Linguist, writer, political activist, and advocate for human rights from the United States.

Of course, we are made in the image and likeness of our Creator. The creative source gave us the ability to co-create our existence. The body is a reflection of our subconscious. That's why self-image plays an important role in defining our self-concept. It's important to make peace with our physical appearance.

It's a sad reality, but most people are not satisfied with their physical appearance. I could almost guarantee that the vast majority of humanity has felt dissatisfied with their appearance at some point in their lives.

As an example: a study[*] conducted in Mexico by the Autonomous University of Baja California with individuals over 18 years old revealed that 84% of participants were dissatisfied with their personal image, with women being more critical than men.

Another study[†] conducted in Chile with university students revealed that 84% of male adolescents and 80% of female adolescents felt dissatisfied with their body image.

An article[‡] recently published in Barcelona by *El País* revealed that more than 60% of the girls interviewed were not happy with their bodies.

These are just a few examples that illustrate a bleak

---

* Casillas Estrella, M.; Montaño Castrejón, N.; Bacardí Gascón, M.; Jiménez Cruz, A. (2007) "Mexicanas con mayor insatisfacción de la imagen corporal," in *Atención Primaria*, 39(2), p. 105.

† Duno, M. & Acosta, E. (2019) "Percepción de la imagen corporal en adolescentes universitarios," in *Revista Chilena de Nutrición*, 46(5), pp. 545-553.

‡ Vallespinós, E. (2024) "Te veo más delgada," in *El País*, available at https://elpais.com/opinion/2024-08-18/te-veo-mas-delgada.html.

reality about our relationship with our bodies. Some argue that the body isn't important, that physical appearance doesn't matter because what truly counts is your spirit. In my opinion, both go hand in hand. A person who is spiritually rich cares for and loves their body because they know everything is interconnected, everything is One.

A healthy mind will undoubtedly manifest in a healthy body. If you have health problems, it's important to look inward and identify which emotions are causing that discomfort.

The Mind-Body Connection

In all fields of science, there is evidence indicating a clear relationship between the mind and the body. Somatization, for example, is a common psychological phenomenon through which unexpressed emotions or stress manifest as physical symptoms such as muscle pain, gastrointestinal issues, nausea, headaches, or chronic fatigue.

The causes are often related to genetic factors, past traumas, the ability to manage emotions, and even cultural factors. The truth is that physical discomfort originates first in the mind. A negative thought about your body—or the circumstances you're in—can trigger physical ailments, even if you don't realize the direct connection between the two.

Other examples can be seen in eating disorders related to body perception. Conditions like bulimia and anorexia arise due to an exaggerated visual distortion of the body.

What causes a person to have such distortions in how they see their body?

Toro Tallero, in his book *The Body as a Crime: Anorexia, Bulimia, Culture, and Society*[*], states that one of the most common causes of such disorders is not only based on genetic or biological factors but also that this body perception is heavily influenced by social and cultural trends.

The social pressure, especially on women, to always have a slim and aesthetically pleasing body causes a psychological disorder that prevents them from enjoying food or their body in a healthy way, as they obsess over counting every calorie they consume.

I, too, have been a victim of this social pressure to always look thin. This pressure doesn't just come from external social expectations; sometimes it starts within the family itself when parents constantly pressure you not to eat food that "makes you fat."

The pressure is severe on women, though it also affects men. The digital entertainment industry also has a significant influence on our psyche. Constant exposure to TV shows and movies where everyone looks like models; following fashion influencers on Instagram or TikTok to copy their diets, workout routines, or plastic surgeries—all with the goal of achieving similar results and a sculpted figure.

---

* Tallero, Toro. *The Body as a Crime: Anorexia, Bulimia, Culture, and Society*. Barcelona: Editorial Ariel, 1996.

I consider it healthy to want to look good, but it crosses the line when a healthy intention turns into a mental disorder. This also applies to the other extreme: the trend of celebrating obesity. Who hasn't come across cases on TikTok where a supposed influencer with some excess weight "shows off" to their followers the extravagant diet that keeps them overweight: in the morning, a giant milkshake with whipped cream; as a snack, a chocolate bar; for lunch, tacos with extra cheese, fries, and an extra portion of bacon; for a snack, a Starbucks drink; and for dinner, a double burger.

In short, I often wonder how these types of influencers —whether those promoting extreme thinness or extreme overweight—gain followers. Is it curiosity? Entertainment? Pity? The most concerning possibility would be if people actually see them as role models.

As popular wisdom says, "All extremes are bad," and when it comes to achieving a good relationship with our body, the ideal is to maintain a proper balance. Become aware of your body, observe it carefully, and decide how you'd like it to look.

What is the reflection in the mirror that would make you feel happy and fulfilled? Once you decide, aim to shape it exactly like that. If you want a slim body and have some excess weight, then commit to achieving the body you visualize. Start acting as if you already have that body: eat the foods you believe that body would consume, do the physical exercise you consider appropriate for that body... and also one you enjoy.

Finding the ideal balance with your body means accepting it unconditionally while recognizing that you have the power to transform it according to how you want to project yourself to the outside world. If you feel comfortable with some extra weight and prefer to enjoy food without too many restrictions, that can also be wonderful, as long as your physical and mental health aren't negatively affected by that decision.

In conclusion, it's about feeling comfortable and fulfilled in your own skin. Achieving that state of well-being is what will allow your connection with your body to function optimally.

In general, our body is designed to fulfill its function. Imbalance comes from toxic thoughts or substances that disrupt its optimal neurochemical state. Our task is to listen to it, pay attention to it, and give it what it needs to provide you with maximum well-being.

The Economy Is a Reflection of Your Home

The economy is represented in the territory where our life unfolds. The dictionary of the Royal Spanish Academy defines economy as "the effective and reasonable administration of goods"; also as "the set of goods and activities that make up the wealth of a community or an individual."

In this context, the economic aspects of your person include, for example, the house you live in, the clothes you wear, your lifestyle, and your relationship with prosperity and money.

In my opinion, I observe that there is a lot of misinformation about economics and personal finances, while many people are uninterested in developing healthy and serious financial education. Multiple factors influence us in developing different types of beliefs about prosperity and money. The most dominant, in my opinion, are cultural, religious, and educational factors. Let's see why.

Culture and Money

In some cultures, money is perceived as something hard to obtain. From a young age, in certain family environments, we're taught that things must be "earned with hard work." Do you remember when, as a child, you wanted a toy you saw in a store window and asked your parents if they'd buy it for you, and they responded with something like, "Money doesn't grow on trees!"?

In Mexico, and in most Latin American countries, we associate earning a lot of money with acts of corruption and dishonesty. I remember occasions in my social circles when we discussed someone who obtained an important position in a company or government. There was always a comment like, "They must have connections," or if someone earned a lot of money, we'd say, "They're probably involved in something shady."

Phrases like "If you don't cheat, you don't get ahead" and "The one who doesn't take advantage struggles" are phrases many of us grew up hearing in our social environments. These kinds of phrases linger in the subconscious, and as a result, people end up developing an unconscious rejection of wealth and earning money because they don't want to be associated with the prejudice of being seen as criminals or bad people.

In other cultures, like the Japanese, collective sentiment and humility are perceived as great social values. Being a person who behaves humbly is considered a fundamental pillar for maintaining harmony in personal relationships. Therefore, displaying attitudes of extravagance and opulence is frowned upon in that society.

The consequence of living with humility is reflected in actions of austerity. Living an austere life means living simply and in harmony with nature. These values, deeply rooted in Japanese society, can be seen in the everyday activities of the Japanese.

I remember when I visited Tokyo a couple of years ago. One of the first things I noticed upon arriving in the city was the level of cleanliness in its streets and public areas. What surprised me even more was realizing there were no trash bins nearby. Incredible! At the time, I wondered how the Japanese managed to keep the streets and places so pristine when they didn't even have trash bins close by.

Shortly after, when I mentioned this to a Japanese colleague, she explained that she was raised at home to avoid generating unnecessary waste and trash at all costs. Therefore, if she generated trash while out, she had to keep it in her bag until she returned home to dispose of it properly. I found it as strange as it was beautiful.

Now I understand where the Kaizen culture, so widespread in Japanese manufacturing, comes from. The Kaizen principles refer to continuous improvement as an essential pillar in companies' competitive strategy. It involves generating value for the customer while reducing resources and practices considered "waste," meaning anything that doesn't add value.

What's interesting about the Kaizen method is that its ultimate goal is to generate wealth, but through a harmonious practice between nature and what adds value for humans. I think this is a balance that makes sense, and if applied wisely, we'd realize that abundance doesn't involve squandering resources recklessly or flaunting opulence, but rather living a harmonious, peaceful, respectful life with the environment while providing everything necessary to live abundantly and with dignity.

Scarcity Mindset vs. Abundance Mindset

One of the most deeply rooted cultural beliefs is that money and resources are limited and that you must guard your money to avoid running out. In these cases, people live in fear of losing money and possessions. If they have a low-paying job, they fear switching to a better-paying one or starting their own business because they're afraid of "losing what's secure."

In my personal experience, I've encountered more

people with a scarcity mindset than those with an abundance mindset. These individuals typically have a deeply ingrained idea that money and resources are limited, unable to see beyond the limits imposed by their mindset.

On one occasion, a middle-aged woman who worked as a clothing and accessories salesperson in a popular shopping mall came to my mentoring session because she wanted to improve her financial situation. She told me:

—"Paola, the truth is I'd like to earn more money. With what I make as a salesperson, I barely cover my monthly bills. I'd love to be able to travel to nice places and buy good clothes without worrying about overdrawing my credit cards."

—"That's a great goal to want to improve your financial situation," I replied. "What actions are you taking to achieve that?"

—"Mmm, well... The truth is I don't have much time to look for another job because I work all day and come home exhausted. I have to pick up my son from daycare and then make dinner. After that, I'm so tired I only have energy to watch a little TV or check my Facebook."

—"I understand how you feel. Have you ever tried replacing your routine of watching TV or checking social media with something that could help you achieve your goal of finding a better-paying job?"

—"Ugh! Honestly, no. I've tried spending some time at night looking for another job, but I'm so exhausted I don't have the energy to think about anything."

As we continued exploring her situation, and I kept

asking questions about modifying her habits to spend less time on TV or social media, she always had an excuse: she argued she didn't have enough energy to think and strategize about finding a better job, or she complained about not having enough money to pay for a course to improve her skills.

The conversations turned into a vicious cycle of not having time, not having enough money, or not having enough energy to change her reality. A mindset that only sees scarcity in every aspect is hard to convince to envision another reality.

How can we tell if we're trapped in a scarcity mindset? Pay attention to your daily thoughts and check if you have any of the following thought patterns:

- You wake up every morning with some worry, whether it's fear that you don't have enough time, money, or resources to do something.
- You feel that giving something to others is a loss for you. For example, if someone asks you for a loan, you think you'll never get that money back.
- You distrust society. You think giving to others brings no benefit because people "just take advantage" of your goodwill.
- You think you're not good enough to earn more money or change your situation.

- You think "the competition is tough" and that's why you can't find a better job or a suitable partner.
- You believe that if you share your knowledge with others, you'll "lose your value."
- You dwell on what your parents or teachers taught you about money; for example, that "money is bad" or that "you have to suffer to deserve it."
- You believe you don't deserve the good things in life. You think you "don't deserve to be happy."
- You believe that being rich is out of your reach because you were born in a certain place, family, or environment. For example, if your parents were humble and you lived in poverty, you're convinced that's your inevitable destiny.
- You tend to victimize yourself. You believe everything bad that happens to you is the fault of your parents, your neighbor, the dog, society, the Andromeda galaxy, climate change... in short, everyone but you.

If you've identified with any of these thought patterns, it's time to take action. First, it's already an achievement to become aware and realize you're trapped in a scarcity mindset. The next step is to work on reprogramming those thoughts or, to paraphrase Joe Dispenza, "rewriting the brain's software" with new thoughts.

Transforming a "Scarcity Mindset" into an "Abundance Mindset"

You can transform your reality and replace those scarcity thoughts with positive, expansive, and vibrant thoughts that will definitely help you achieve the life you desire.

Start by gradually introducing these types of thoughts into your life. The ideal approach is to begin slowly but consistently, becoming aware and starting to reframe those deeply rooted negative thoughts that, in most cases, are generated automatically.

When you wake up each morning, try to notice the thought or feeling you perceive at that moment and say to yourself: "Today is a wonderful day. I have the power to improve my life." Close your eyes for a moment and imagine yourself as that ideal person, the person you aspire to be. How does that person breathe? How do they walk? How do they dress? What would their ideal morning routine be?

At first, you don't have to act immediately. The important thing is to start slowly and transform your reality gradually. First, focus on clearly imagining that person. Take a few minutes to visualize that perfect morning. Once you see and feel it, you'll notice you start to smile and breathe more deeply and consciously. Your mind calms and aligns with that new image. Once you've managed to visualize it and can smile at that new "you" you're envisioning, you can stop the exercise and return to your usual routine.

You'll see that if you repeat this visualization every morning, even if you dedicate just a couple of minutes a day, you'll notice that you'll gradually start transforming that reality. Your subconscious will slowly adapt to the new reality and project those actions into your conscious state.

And so, with every event that happens during the day, you can repeat the same exercise: close your eyes for a moment and imagine: What would my ideal day be like? How do I behave with others? How do I observe the world around me? What thoughts do I have about money and my possessions? How do I interact with my work colleagues? What kind of food do I choose to nourish myself?

Gradually becoming aware of which thoughts dominate you, which actions you take based on those thoughts, and consistently replacing them little by little will inevitably lead you to become the person you've visualized.

When you've managed to replace a scarcity mindset with an abundance mindset, you'll realize that:

- Money is simply a means to achieve your goals. The energy you give to money is the energy money returns to your life.

- You start acting like an abundant person: you smile, walk, and speak with complete calm. There's nothing to worry about because everything is already resolved.
- You know you can only help others to the extent that you're able to help yourself.
- You realize that investing in yourself, your businesses, and your work generates more opportunities and abundance than thinking only about saving and doing everything as cheaply as possible.
- You know that in the reality in which the world operates, resources are unlimited.
- You know that what you give to others, you're actually giving to yourself.
- You understand that there will always be new opportunities. Failures don't limit you; they open doors to many other opportunities.
- You improve your personal relationships because your heart and thoughts are generous, expansive, and grateful. You'll attract the right people like honey attracts bees.

The abundant mindset can be achieved, just as any aspect of life can be achieved when you invest time, love, focus, and practice. How do elite athletes prepare for a competition? How do the world's best chefs prepare their most valued dishes? How does a company become successful and gain many clients? How does a person transform their body from being overweight to a healthy, slim, and strong body?

Everything operates under the same logic. Miracles happen in broad daylight, in front of us, and at all times. The only thing we have to do is deeply accept this truth and realize that we are the ones who create miracles. It's in our nature as genies.

> *"A joyful heart makes a cheerful face, but a sad heart breaks the spirit."*
>
> — Proverbs 15:13

Religion and Money

Religion can significantly influence how we relate to economic and financial matters. In some branches of Christianity, the idea is propagated that "money is the root of all evil." An example can be found in Matthew 19:23-24, which reads: "Then Jesus said to his disciples, 'Truly I tell you, it is hard for a rich person to enter the kingdom of heaven. Again I tell you, it is easier for a camel to go through the eye of a needle than for a rich person to enter the kingdom of God.'" Or "Better a little with the fear of the Lord than great wealth with turmoil" (Proverbs 15:16).

These types of phrases cause confusion among believers. Many may come to associate these phrases with the idea that loving money is bad and that money is of the devil. When religion becomes an ideology that leads to fanaticism, it's difficult for a person to realize that Bible passages should never be taken literally.

The Christian religion is the religion that built the West, and Western culture is one of the most advanced and prosperous civilizations. It's important not to interpret certain Bible passages or the beliefs of its preachers literally, as they often use religion as a tool for control rather than as a belief system with which a society identifies to materialize the common good.

Another example is in Islam, where Islamic banking, despite being declared "non-religious," bases its fundamental principles on Sharia.* For instance, Islam prohibits interest (*riba*). This means the bank does not offer loans with an interest rate as traditional banks do. According to this principle, the concept of interest rates is incompatible with the concept of equity practiced in Islam.

In an economic context, this means that borrowing money from a bank is very difficult (if not impossible) in Islamic states, making it harder for families or businesses to access any type of bank loan.

According to the ethics of finance based on the teachings of the Quran, Muslims believe that profits should be based on justice and equality of opportunity rather than individual outcomes. Therefore, Islamic banks and finan-

---

* Sharia, or Islamic law, consists of a set of rules governing the public and private life of the Muslim population. The word "Sharia" can be translated as "the path of Islam" and is based on the teachings of the Quran. For more information, see https://elordenmundial.com/que-es-sharia-ley-islamica/.

cial institutions support income redistribution to provide a minimum income level for those with limited resources, known as *zakat*.

In this context, a person with deeply rooted Islamic beliefs will think that capitalism—or earning money based on individual merit—is something that goes against the Quran and is therefore bad.

Another example is in Buddhism. Buddhism emphasizes material detachment for ultimate personal fulfillment (*Nirvana*). This could trigger feelings of repulsion toward money and material possessions, although the Buddhist religion itself does not condemn money as inherently negative.

According to the teachings of Buddha, money itself is a neutral medium. What you do with money determines whether the karma will be positive or negative. Do you use money to do good in society? To make the people around you happy? Or do you use it to satisfy your own ego?

I could continue listing examples of how religion profoundly influences our beliefs about money and material possessions, but I believe the point is already clear.

Education and Money

The education system, of course, plays a leading role in how we relate to money. Of the more than twenty years we spend immersed in different levels of schooling, none of them teach us how to manage money and personal finances.

Even careers like Business Administration, Accounting, Finance, and Economics are not taught in a way that the average student can apply something meaningful to manage their own finances. I count myself among those students who, despite earning a Master's in International Business, graduated without any idea of how to manage my money.

There was a strange cognitive dissonance. On one hand, during my university years, I studied accounting, finance, business administration, economics, industrial development, among many other subjects that, in theory, should have made me an expert in managing money. But on the other hand, my mind didn't connect what I learned in the classroom with my personal life... as if they were two parallel worlds that never touched!

In class, I learned all the rules and technicalities of economic theories. At home, I didn't even think about having financial planning. I practiced the basics: from the little I earned, I tried to save ten percent, a goal I rarely achieved because, being young and earning your own money, you think more about what to spend it on than what to invest it in.

My family wasn't a good example of financial management either. It wasn't until I started paying attention to the topic of finances that I realized the education I'd had up to that point was very limited. For example, I didn't understand passive income investments. I didn't know how to manage my time in relation to money. I thought the more I worked, the more money I should earn. I had no idea about salary negotiations. I didn't know what managing retirement investment funds or real estate investments meant... in short.

Basically, I was barely surviving on my salary, thinking the only way to earn money was to find a good job, work hard, climb the ranks, and eventually hope for salary increases, which—as I later learned—don't come easily or frequently.

In essence, having a job and earning a salary isn't a wrong way to make money. In fact, it's one of the first experiences we have when we start earning money independently. Any job is an act of service to others that should be compensated.

The problem arises when we get stuck in a particular belief about how to generate money. It took me a while to understand that generating money isn't a science you can learn with mathematical formulas, memorizing technicalities, or years of studying economics.

Money is made first in the mind. As Morgan Housel states in his book *The Psychology of Money*, "Financial success is not a hard science. It's actually a personal skill, where behavior and belief are more important than what you know."

I'm convinced this comes very close to the truth. Education teaches us about money the same way it teaches us chemistry, mathematics, history, and more. We only learn about laws and rules. What we don't learn is the psychology behind money. The emotions, beliefs, and what truly drives the use of money in everyday life.

Isn't it interesting that despite the finance, economics, and accounting courses taught to millions of students worldwide, from public universities to the most prestigious ones like Harvard, Princeton, and others, the majority of the population still has financial problems?

How many people do you know who studied Finance as a career and are millionaires? I know very few cases, and those few are people who started their own business and managed to expand and capitalize it, but not necessarily thanks to the formal education they received in school and university.

In summary, the vision we develop about money has its deepest roots in personal experiences and the social, historical, and cultural context in which we grow up. We cannot expect a person who grew up in a precarious household, in conditions of severe poverty, to view money the same way as someone who grew up in an environment full of privileges.

Nor can we expect the financial theories taught in school to apply to everyone in the same way. Every decision a person makes about money is justified by the information they had at the time and considered the best option, based on how they see the world according to their mental model.

These people may be completely uninformed, or they may have all the information in the world. They may be bad at math, or they may be excellent. They may know what they're doing or have no idea. They may be swayed by cheap marketing or social media. Perhaps they seek to copy their favorite idol or influencer of the moment. They may misjudge the consequences of their actions. Depending on how they see the world and their mindset, the consequences will manifest in the external world.

I'll provide an example of how mindset shapes decisions and affects personal finances: I used to think that saving up to buy a Louis Vuitton bag to show off on the streets was a symbol of success, but now I consider it a financial mistake.

Investing in that bag (which costs an average of about 1,400 euros) didn't result in generating more profits. I could sell it, but I won't recover the return on investment because it has a depreciation value. On the contrary, investing those 1,400 euros in a Neuro-Sales or Marketing course would offer a return.

Acquiring a new skill becomes an asset I can capitalize on. I can recover the return on investment because, thanks to the course, my market value increases, allowing me to generate more added value with my work and quickly recover the invested money.

What I want to emphasize here is not to motivate you to think in a specific way about money and material possessions, nor do I want to convince you not to study Economics or Finance at university.

I believe it's important to make it clear that education

has a significant influence on how you feel and think about money. And if we want to free our genie from mental limitations, we must broaden our horizons, observe the bars of the mental prison, understand that we're inside, and see that there are infinite possibilities to break out and live in abundance and prosperity.

Chapter 6

The Creative and Sexual Self: Doing

"Sexuality is the creative energy of all genius. There has never been, nor will there ever be, a great leader, builder, or artist who lacks that driving force of sex."

—Napoleon Hill

In his book *Think and Grow Rich*, Napoleon Hill argues that sexual energy is one of the most powerful motivators for stimulating the mind to reach heightened states of vibration. These states unlock the door to creative imagination, enthusiasm, and intense desire.

This makes a lot of sense to me. Humans are born with the seed of reproductive instinct. Entire civilizations have been built thanks to this innate drive to create life. This vital force of reproduction has inspired humans to build homes, buildings, cities, and industries to support the desire to populate the planet.

Sexual energy sparks imagination. I remember my teenage years, spending hours daydreaming about romantic stories with my crushes. I'd pour so much energy into imagining places where I might run into them. I wrote poems dedicated to my first loves.

I was literally "living in the clouds," in a parallel world where anything was possible. And what was my greatest wish? To feel loved in return. To feel like I could have a relationship where we could build something beautiful together—even if it was just a love story.

When transformed into sexual energy, love becomes a powerful cocktail that can change lives. The emotion of love nurtures and develops our creative and artistic nature. The traces of true love linger in the human heart forever.

The Driving Force of Great Leaders

When I studied the lives of leaders I admired for my book *The Success Mindset*, I noticed a common trait: at some point, they were inspired by their partners.

Take Steve Jobs, co-founder of Apple. In his autobiography, he credited his wife, Laurene, for his return to leading the company. She was a source of inspiration and emotional support, influencing many of his business decisions and innovative products.

Another example is John Lennon. His relationship with Yoko Ono was one of the most controversial and iconic of its time. In Ray Coleman's biography, *Lennon: The Definitive Biography*, it's said that Yoko inspired John to explore new forms of musical expression and was a key influence in launching his solo career.

When Marie Curie began her research on radioactivity, she faced countless obstacles, from skeptical scientists to societal prejudices. Yet her husband, Pierre Curie, a respected scientist, encouraged her to keep going. He supported her unconditionally, and together they discovered radium and polonium.

I could list countless celebrities who attribute their success to the inspiration of a partner or a youthful love. As the saying goes, "Behind every great man is a great woman," or equally, "Behind every great woman is a great man."

Imagine a world without Shakespeare, Mozart, or great painters like Leonardo da Vinci or Pablo Picasso. Or, closer to our time, the brilliant Japanese artist Yayoi Kusama or American gymnast Simone Biles. These timeless artists continue to inspire us with their immortal works. Such creations are only possible when a sublime force burns within you—a devotion to love, life, and art.

Art is a way to express human ideas, feelings, and emotions. It's a way to channel sexual energy into the physical world through paintings, poems, music, sculptures, or even business ideas and social movements.

Misconceptions About Sex

In our culture, we often talk about sex negatively. Throughout history, societies have treated sex as a taboo topic, not to be discussed at family dinners or in social settings.

This repression of sex has led to destructive behaviors. Instead of seeing sex as a natural act of creation—pure life energy—it's often viewed as something to be ashamed of.

People with high sexual energy—magnetic individuals—can feel attacked by those who don't understand that suppressing one of nature's most powerful forces harms us.

Austrian physician, psychoanalyst, and scientist Wilhelm Reich spent years studying the link between neurosis and sexual repression. He argued that neurotic anxiety arises from a mix of apprehension and suppressed sexual energy.

The devastating consequences of treating sex as dangerous, mundane, or perverse can be seen throughout history in oppressive religious manipulation and, today, in the trend of "hypersexualization."

We've separated love from sex, even though they come from the same source and are intertwined. Sex in our society has been reduced to a tool for mass control, manipulation, and marketing.

We no longer "make love"; we "have sex." The mystery, seduction, and sweet anticipation are gone. Everything is rushed now, with no time for romance. Sex has become just another transaction.

Don't believe me? Look at apps like Tinder, where you can swipe through thousands of "potential matches" like you're choosing from a menu or picking shoes from a catalog. Then there are platforms like OnlyFans or influencers like Bonnie Blue, who gained fame after claiming to have slept with over a thousand men in under twelve hours.

Social media is flooded with influencers selling sexual content. In the past, if a man wanted to be with a woman, he had to make an effort: court her, go on dates, get to know her friends, and wait patiently for the right moment —if he was lucky enough not to wait until marriage.

Now, neither men nor women need any of that. They can "consume" sex through a screen without leaving home. Or, the bolder ones can meet someone from Tinder for a "one-night stand."

The absurdity is that, even though sex is more accessible than ever, people are having less of it. Here are some interesting findings:

- A study by the William James Research Center in Portugal found that excessive use of social media and smartphones is linked to reduced sexual desire and even decreased sexual function in both men and women. In men, this includes issues like erectile dysfunction and difficulty reaching orgasm.
- An article in the digital version of *El País* (Spain) noted that younger generations are less

interested in sexual relationships, prioritizing friendships, influencers, or virtual crushes instead.
- A recent study in the UK* showed a decline in partnered sexual activity due to excessive smartphone use.

This doesn't surprise me anymore. We're following in the footsteps of societies like Japan, where this "sexless epidemic" has been growing for years.

When I visited Japan a few years ago, I was shocked to see huge gaming arcades where people went to play video games. One day, out of curiosity, I stepped into one. The place was massive, packed with all kinds of games, and full of people—mostly men—sitting alone in front of screens. I'd never felt such loneliness in a place so loud, crowded, and yet so empty.

It was around 7 p.m., and the arcade was already packed with people who likely went there after work. It felt surreal to me. Moving from the computer screen at work to the screen of a video game? No wonder the Japanese have fewer sexual relationships with a routine like that!

Could it be that these technologies are another weapon working against us knowing ourselves better?

---

* Source: https://www.abc.es/tecnologia/informatica/soluciones/abci-telefono-tiene-culpa-tengas-menos-sexo-201905082332_noticia.html, accessed March 31, 2025.

Wilhelm Reich warned us in his book *The Murder of Christ*: "The well-known signs of genital frustration—impure thoughts, lust, cruelty, whether direct or moralistic with false kindness—are absurd in the image of Christ. [...] Christ could not have been pure as a stream and sharp as a deer if he had been filled with the filth of perverted sexuality due to the frustration of natural contact. Without a doubt: Christ knew love in the body and with women, as he knew so many other natural things."

Sexual repression—whether from religion, education, or social norms—has distanced us from a natural relationship with our bodies. Sexuality is an act of love that happens spontaneously and naturally. We don't need to force anything. We don't need to follow foolish doctrines. We don't need to fall into depravity. And we certainly don't need to feel ashamed of our vibrant, beautiful, radiant sexual energy.

Connecting Healthily with Our Sexual Energy

Experts like Cal Newport and Carol Dweck say one reason most people don't achieve success before their 40s is that success often comes from years of practice, a growth mindset, and maturity. American author Robert Greene also points to a key factor: channeling energy effectively.

After studying thousands of entrepreneurs across industries, Napoleon Hill noticed that most achieved "success" between their 40s and 50s. He attributed this to people learning to channel their sexual energy in healthier, more productive ways than in their youth.

Hill argued that, before their 40s, many people focus too much on dissipating their sexual energy through physical indulgence—spending too much time thinking about sex and satisfying their urges. Most don't realize at that age that the urgency of sex can be channeled into other possibilities beyond physical expression.

That's why, in their youth, many men and women pour energy into partying, dating, or having multiple partners, not realizing that energy could be directed toward creating great works that shape their life's purpose.

Sexual energy is powerful. When used to our advantage, it can free us from the "rigid armor" that holds us back. How do we break free? By accepting that you are a sensual person with a wonderful connection to nature. Embracing this from your soul makes you magnetic.

Have you ever met someone who instantly draws you in? I'm not talking about physical beauty but something in their gaze, their smile, their walk that you can't stop admiring.

A magnetic person is a natural person. They attract others with their charisma. Their energy is high, and their presence lights up every room. Here are a few signs of a highly magnetic person:

- **Tone of Voice**: A clear, well-modulated voice. A deep, steady tone conveys authority and confidence, while a high, melodic voice can feel sweet and charming.

- **Handshake**: A firm handshake signals magnetism.
- **Posture**: Magnetic people move with grace, fluidity, and ease—not stiff or nervous.
- **Style**: They choose clothes that flatter them and enhance their appeal.
- **Thought Vibration**: This one's fascinating. People with strong sexual energy often blend the emotion of sex with their thoughts. This can be incredibly powerful, especially in sales —it's the art of pure seduction.

It's no surprise that highly seductive people succeed in their personal and professional lives. Think of the leaders, speakers, or artists you admire. They captivate you with how they express themselves, think, or look. They remind you of your natural state of being, even if unconsciously. Wilhelm Reich describes this beautifully:

"The genital embrace arises naturally from a total bodily impulse that slowly builds into a desire to merge with another body. You can see this fundamental trait in birds, frogs, butterflies, snails, deer, and other animals living freely. The final pleasure of total energy release in orgasm is the spontaneous result of prolonged small pleasures."

A person in harmony with their reproductive nature acts with the power of faith. They trust their natural senses. They feel their body fully and aren't frustrated by "limitations" because they understand they have none. They don't see their body as just a piece of flesh to satisfy and then feel guilty about.

A person doesn't "try to be" a person—they simply *are*. To me, that's the power of feeling this creative life force, given by the source of creation, God, or whatever you choose to call it. Like birds, flowers, olive trees, lions, and dolphins know how to *be*, the creative source is in everything—not a figure to worship.

The Kingdom of God is the kingdom of love and creation. So, remember: your genie is inherently sexual. Sexuality is simply an expression of life force, a symbol of creativity and imagination.

Creative energy is fire, mystery, and life itself. So, shed that armor. Stop believing in the repressive tyranny that keeps you from enjoying who you are. Embrace your sexual energy... and unleash your genie.

Chapter 7

From Self-Criticism to Self-Compassion: How to Change the Conversation with Yourself

To wrap up this second part, I'd like to share a short guide to help you heal your relationship with yourself and manage that inner voice of self-criticism and perfectionism, which does nothing to support your personal fulfillment.

1. Review Your Goals: Are They Realistic?

This is the first step toward self-sabotage. We love setting impossible goals. I'm not saying you should aim low, but you need to set goals that match your abilities.

In my mentoring sessions, I've noticed this is where many clients get frustrated. They come to me upset because they can't meet the goals they set for themselves. Once, a young woman shared how discouraged she felt because she couldn't stick to the "perfect" routines she saw on Instagram reels: women waking up at 5 a.m., hitting the gym, eating a boiled egg and salad for breakfast, working eight hours straight, jogging with their dog, blending a fresh fruit smoothie, and then doing a nightly beauty routine.

"How can I not keep up with that influencer's routine?" she complained. I've addressed in my other books how dangerous it can be to use social media as a measure of reality. One downside of these platforms is that they create a parallel world, often completely out of touch with real life.

Many people don't realize that behind the lives of top influencers is a production team, like in a movie. That influencer who seems to live a "normal life" with powerful daily habits is often filming a scene for their personal blockbuster.

Even if their routines are real, do you really want to copy someone else's habits exactly? Wouldn't it make more sense to design routines that fit *your* life's unique circumstances?

No goal or routine is inherently better or worse. A routine is only powerful if it improves *your* life. Waking up at 5 a.m. every day isn't magical on its own. Its value comes from what you do with that time and why it matters to you.

The smartest approach is to set personal goals based on what's most important to you and your circumstances. If you have young kids, a demanding job, or a sick family member to care for, it's not realistic to follow the routines of trendy influencers who likely don't have those responsibilities. Their job is to make money by grabbing your attention!

Here's a simple but effective method for setting realistic goals: Grab a blank sheet of paper and a pen. Write down what you want to achieve in the medium to long term (say, 5 to 10 years). List at least 5 goals, up to 10. Then, think about short-term actions that will help you reach those long-term goals. Write down at least one action per goal. Finally, ask yourself: *What can I do today to move closer to my goals?*

Let's say one of your goals is to save money for a new car. A short-term action could be saving 5% of your monthly income. Now, ask: *What can I do today to save that 5% by the end of the month?* Maybe you analyze your daily expenses and decide to make coffee at home instead of buying it at Starbucks or cook lunch instead of eating out.

The key is to choose daily actions that are realistic for your life and align with your personal goals.

2. Be Flexible with Yourself (and Others)

People who are rigid with themselves can't handle failure. They tend to be perfectionists and have a low tolerance for frustration. It's no surprise they're stressed all the time. The world never meets their expectations—everyone else seems to mess up, and nothing is ever good enough.

I know people like this. It's like the world doesn't deserve them. From the moment they wake up, they complain about everything: the coffee's not hot enough, people drive terribly, no one at the office knows anything, coworkers do everything wrong, the kids don't listen, it's too hot or too cold, and on and on.

We love judging and labelling everything in black-and-white terms. It's either good or bad, smart or stupid. But the world is full of shades of gray, so you can't judge things so harshly—reality doesn't work that way.

If you're a perfectionist, try to understand what's behind your obsession with doing everything perfectly. Chances are, you're afraid of being seen as incompetent or incapable. You become your own worst critic.

That fear of not doing things well spills outward. You're not just intolerant of your own mistakes but also of others'. This can push people away—they've got enough problems without dealing with someone who can't listen or understand.

Perfectionism is an imaginary place born from the ego. It's a shield we hide behind to avoid judgment. But it paralyzes action and stifles creativity.

If you're a perfectionist, try this little experiment: for one week, shake up your schedule. Skip your usual rituals. Wake up earlier or later than normal. Take a different route to work. Try a meal you wouldn't usually pick. Compliment someone you usually criticize or judge as "useless." See what happens.

You'll likely find the world keeps spinning. You might even learn something new. Maybe you discover a less congested route to work or realize that "useless" person has some great ideas. You might find a new favorite dish. Don't be afraid of change!

To be clear, I'm not saying you should abandon your routines forever. If they work for you and bring good results, stick with them. But being rigidly attached to them stops you from finding new ways to see and do things. In a fast-changing world, keeping an open mind is key.

3. Practice Positive Self-Talk

The saying "You're your own worst critic" exists for a reason. We tend to be incredibly hard on ourselves, constantly judging ourselves harshly through our inner dialogue.

Why is it so hard to talk to ourselves with love and respect? I suspect it's a habit we pick up in childhood. If your parents were overly strict or you faced bullying from siblings or classmates, part of your subconscious might have accepted those harsh words as true—and you still believe them as an adult.

The truth is, the only person who can break that cycle of negative self-talk is *you*. You have to make peace with your inner self, which is perfect and divine in its essence. We've forgotten that making mistakes is part of being human—a natural process meant to help us grow and improve.

Harshly criticizing yourself for your mistakes, appearance, or life circumstances only attracts more of the same. If you've read my previous books, you know I believe our reality is just energy decoded by our brain. What you see as "the world out there" is just your perception, quantum information your brain interprets from your unique perspective.

If you've spent years telling yourself you're a "failure," "poor," or "useless at everything," it's no wonder you attract negative experiences like a magnet.

I know some people are skeptical of the idea that reality is shaped by consciousness, not matter. They believe the physical world exists on its own, and humanity is just a pawn in a giant chess game, subject to random luck or tragedy.

My goal isn't to convince you one way or another. Instead, I invite you to try this experiment: for one full day, only say positive things to yourself. Look in the mirror and be generous with your words.

Treat yourself, for just one day, with the respect and care you'd give someone you truly admire. Thank yourself for all the effort you put into living your best life, given your abilities at each moment. Listen to yourself, have an open and loving inner dialogue. Try it for a day and notice how you feel by the end.

When I did this experiment with some clients, they told me they felt renewed, like a new energy had taken over. Suddenly, they wanted to socialize more, smile at strangers, and, as one client put it, "I felt so light, like my body didn't weigh me down."

Positive words are the most beautiful resonance in the universe.

4. Build Strong Self-Esteem—Fall in Love with Yourself

Most of us swing between love and hate, often leaning more toward self-hate than self-love. Healthy love makes you feel complete, at peace, and in harmony with your life and the world around you. It's not full of drama or insecurity.

Your social and family environment, especially in childhood, plays a huge role in shaping your self-esteem. Absent parents might have left you feeling unloved, or overly strict parents might have been cold in showing their affection. The wounds we carry from childhood linger in our subconscious, quietly influencing the relationships we form as adults.

That's why we need to be aware of our self-concept. Learning to love and accept ourselves unconditionally is the first step out of neurosis.

Why is it so hard to love ourselves? I think we learn to suppress who we truly are, replacing our authentic self with a social mask. We become what our parents, teachers, and society expect us to be. We bury our true selves.

Over time, we start believing that mask *is* who we are. But in tough or pivotal moments, we face an existential crisis:

WHO AM I? IS THIS THE LIFE I WANT? IS THIS THE PERSON I WANT TO BE?

When we confront these questions, we might realize we're not who we thought. Something intangible inside us demands to be expressed. Identity crises happen because a deep, immaterial energy within you is protesting, yearning to be set free.

Your trapped genie, chained to a rigid body and mindset, is begging to break out. This creates a battle. Your true energy—the love you *are*—clashes with the rigid, mechanical, limited shell you've built as your "persona."

The ego, that outer shell, fights to survive. It wants you to believe the shell matters most, that appearances and social status are everything.

The ego knows that freeing your genie means its own end. That rigid shell keeps us from seeing who we truly are. But when we let our genie out, we raise our consciousness to higher levels. We let creative energy take over, and that's when miracles happen.

Dr. Joe Dispenza calls this transcending "the big three": the body (your personal shell), the environment (the collective shell), and time (the universal shell). When your consciousness focuses so intensely on the present moment, you forget who you are, where you are, and even lose track of time.

You've probably felt this when doing something you love. Time vanishes, and you "merge" with the activity, becoming one with it. For me, this happens with writing. When I write and fully surrender to it, everything else fades away. My subconscious takes over, and I just enjoy the act of writing.

Sometimes, when I reread what I've written, I'm amazed. I don't always remember writing certain things. I think it's because I was so immersed in the moment that it flowed from my subconscious without me noticing.

To circle back to self-concept, loving yourself is about surrendering to who you are in all your dimensions. If I can make that message clear, I'll be satisfied.

Embracing who we are helps us face life's challenges with calm and less stress, without rigidity or neurosis. There's no shell to protect—just the joy of *being*.

How do we know if we're stuck in low-vibration energies that push us toward survival versus higher energies that bring us closer to creation? I love Dr. Joe Dispenza's "Survival vs. Creation" chart, which I've included as an appendix at the end of this book. Another similar and equally fascinating scale is Dr. David Hawkins' from his book *Power vs. Force*. Both measure consciousness in similar ways.

Dispenza's scale shows that a body in survival mode operates at low energy vibrations, experiencing stress, imbalance, and illness. A body focused on creative energy is healthy, naturally regenerating, and filled with love, acceptance, and joy.

Hawkins' map of consciousness ranks energy frequencies from low to high: apathy, indifference, and resentment are the lowest; courage is the turning point, leading to vibrant energies like reason, acceptance, and, ultimately, love—the highest vibrational energy known to humanity.

We can conclude that self-love is the path to reconciling with our existence and opens the door to incredible destinations aligned with our truth.

5. Celebrate Your Wins

Every personal victory, no matter how small, deserves celebration. Many of us get caught up in others' achievements. When someone shares their success, we might feel a mix of unease or disappointment—not because of their win, but because we wish *we* were the ones getting that attention or praise.

Let's be honest: most people don't like seeing others do better than them. It's sad, but it's true. Relying on others' approval or praise to feel important or accomplished is a waste of time and energy.

The only person who can pull you out of that emotional marathon is *you*. Your perception shapes your world. Celebrating your wins, from the smallest to the biggest, is your responsibility. I'm not saying don't share them with others, but first, feel fulfilled and happy with yourself without needing external validation.

This is especially important when working toward long-term dreams or goals. Day-to-day progress might feel invisible, like you're stuck in the same old routine. But focused daily action shapes reality bit by bit until, one day, the change becomes clear.

Having a healthy relationship with your achievements is key to a fulfilling, balanced life. We get distracted by the unconscious race to "have it all" compared to others.

When you see someone buy a new house, finish a degree, reach their ideal weight, or land their dream job, you might focus too much on their success. You start thinking negatively about yourself, comparing their wins to yours. Sometimes, these comparisons don't even make sense, but we do it anyway.

It's crucial to break free from that comparison spiral, which social media has only made worse. Here's a challenge: forget the need to show off your achievements to others or post them online—your dream vacation, your first gym visit, that almond milk latte from Starbucks, your latest diploma.

When you achieve something you're proud of, take a quiet moment with your eyes closed to thank yourself deeply for it.

Thank God for giving you the chance to grow and experience enriching moments. Thank your higher self for guiding you every step of the way. Thank life and celebrate every detail of your win with intensity. Savor the beautiful feeling of being happy for fulfilling a personal desire.

Take time to celebrate alone. Treat yourself to a small indulgence—a chocolate, a spa visit, a glass of good wine, a massage, whatever you love. Savor the victory and live it as fully as you can.

You'll notice that celebrating your wins privately reduces the urge to "show off" to others. You might even feel like you don't need to broadcast them at all. And if you do share, you'll care less about others' reactions. Try it and let me know how it goes—it's worked wonders for me.

The difference between being ordinary and extraordinary comes down to two simple syllables: *extra*. It takes a bit more effort, but it makes all the difference. Doing things with care turns you into a person of high value. Sometimes, it's not about doing a lot—just a little more. That small extra effort can change everything.

Stay centered. If you stay true to your essence, the world will bring you peace and calm. When we focus on what matters, without the noise of seeking attention, the power of unity helps us fulfill our true destiny, living in the same creative energy.

"He who has a why to live for can bear almost any how."
—Friedrich Nietzsche

Part Three

Healing Relationships

Even though we're a social species, used to living in communities since the dawn of time, I still don't understand why we haven't made significant progress in how we relate to one another. Why do we keep falling into conflict over and over again?

What's curious to me is that the closer a relationship is, the bigger the conflicts seem to get. It's pretty normal to go out in public and be polite with strangers in transactional, superficial interactions (though sometimes, not even that).

But as soon as relationships get closer—think mother and child, spouses, partners, or close friends—emotions intensify. We're more likely to feel bursts of anger, frustration, or aggression toward them.

I tend to think the problem lies in the fear of being

exposed. Someone who knows you well can see past the "mask," that ego you build to shield yourself from the world. That vulnerability—the terror of being truly seen—lashes out to protect its status quo.

Why do we get stuck in the stubborn need to always be right? In the win-lose mindset, everyone loses.

Another issue we haven't solved is our obsession with simplifying the complexity of our relationships. To our ego, relationships can be measured in a linear and binary way: linear in the sense that a relationship can only get better or worse, and binary in judging it between two extremes—you treat me well or you treat me poorly; you meet my expectations or you don't.

When you judge in a binary way—good or bad, fat or thin, black or white—it inevitably leads to conflict with the other person. We have this stubborn habit of wanting to classify everything, but a person's nature is far from binary or linear. We don't go through life collecting zeros and ones!

In my view, just as life can't be explained or find transcendence in a linear or binary way, the same applies to human relationships. You can't capture the multidimensionality of a person with a couple of elementary-school math parameters.

No one is entirely good or entirely bad. No one will ever perfectly match the expectations of your illusions or ego. That's why, when we start a relationship expecting binary, linear results, we end up suffering, thinking love isn't for us or that we'll never be truly understood.

The only fundamental law I believe in is that all relationships have two primary foundations: those based on love and those based on fear. When you choose to love, you don't expect linear behavior from someone. You accept that your endless list of expectations will never be fully met. You accept that your partner snores, has smelly feet, or chews loudly (even if you keep pointing it out).

You also accept that relationships are, as author Raimon Samsó puts it, a "gallery of mirrors." Every relationship reflects your own shortcomings or excesses.

Relationships are a journey of learning to love. Each one offers a chance to discover what true love has to offer. True love comes from a deeper acceptance that transcends dualities.

It's worth considering this: we are multidimensional beings. A person is both good and bad at the same time. We all have moments when we feel happy and charming, but we also carry the potential to explode in anger or sink into deep sadness.

It's like quantum physics: a wave is both a particle and a wave, depending on when you observe it. At one moment, your partner might be the sweetest person alive, and three minutes later, they're furious or in tears. It's not that they're bipolar—it's just the multidimensional nature of being human.

Loving truly means accepting someone fully. You

choose to love despite the things you don't like or the expectations they don't meet. Of course, this assumes healthy love, which respects boundaries, avoids physical or emotional harm, and honors individuality.

Love based on fear comes from our need to classify and judge according to our expectations. Any action that challenges the ego is likely to be rejected, sparking conflict with the person who supposedly caused it. So, we love with conditions: "You scratch my back, I scratch yours." I love you only if you meet my requirements—take me to dinner every Friday, buy me flowers, be there when I'm down, stay in a good mood, have interesting conversations, dress well, walk well... and so on, endlessly.

But the moment something isn't met, my love crashes. I might question if I still love you or maybe I don't. The romanticism of illusory love is a need. And need is the absence of true love. The bigger the ego, the less peace and the more suffering.

That's why the idea of romantic love has hurt millions of couples who've fallen for Hollywood-style fantasies. Many break off relationships when the binary equation doesn't add up because their fear of losing outweighs their desire to love.

Relationships don't have to be complicated if we just understand this: the act of loving attracts the feeling. Love is the result of choosing to love first. Believing love comes before you decide to love is a dangerous fantasy. Choose to love—it's worth the risk.

In the coming chapters, we'll explore the dimensions

of true love and how we can apply them to heal personal relationships and, ultimately, transform the world around us.

> *"If nothing saves us from death, at least let love save us from life."*
>
> —Pablo Neruda

Chapter 8

The Dimensions of Love

"What the heart gives, it never loses."
—Fyodor Dostoevsky

In this life, we express love in at least three fundamental dimensions: love for ourselves, which is the core from which everything else flows. We can't truly perceive love if we've never felt some form of love for ourselves.

When we come into this world, we instinctively sense that our existence has value, so we fight to survive. We seek food, warmth, and protection at all costs. Our cries and early survival instincts are our first signs of self-love.

Over time, we experience love for family and those close to us. Looking into our mother's eyes unlocks the mystery of infinite love. In the eyes of young children, you can see the miracle of true love reflected. A child's first great love is for their parents. Later, they learn to love their siblings and other family members, though in different ways and degrees.

Then comes our first romantic love. It's the first time men and women experience new shades of love. Through the existence of another, we discover the grandeur and beauty of life. Romantic love is a moment of ecstasy where, for the first time, we feel a desire to step outside ourselves. We realize there's a feeling that transcends and surpasses us.

The next level of love extends to the world—our social interactions, love for our community, pride in belonging to a homeland, or even loving humanity itself simply for sharing existence.

I believe human love evolves through these stages, and it can't be any other way. You can't love humanity without first loving and accepting yourself. You can't give what you don't have. Love always starts from within.

So, in my view, to achieve complete healing, we must consider these dimensions. You can't love humanity without first having a healthy relationship with your parents, siblings, and family. How can someone claim to love humanity but despise their parents? How can someone say they love their partner while destroying themselves? In love, there are no contradictions.

For love to be authentic, it must have these characteristics:

1. Trust

Trust is a way of feeling completely certain that things will work out and take the course they're meant to for your full realization. Love requires a deep knowing that everything you desire will come to be—that it's a latent reality in a parallel plane, reachable if you believe in it.

As described in *A Course in Miracles* by American psychologist Helen Schucman, "God's teachers trust in the world because they've learned it's not governed by the laws the world made up. It's governed by a power within them, but not of them."

When we don't trust ourselves (or others), it's because we fear losing something in the exchange of expectations. Not trusting someone simply means you're afraid they won't meet the expectations you've created.

In true love, there's no such thing as mistrust. There's no fear of loss because, deep in your being, you know you already have everything you need to live a full life.

Building trust also involves changing how we see the world's events. It's about realizing that everything that happens in your life—whether you see it as positive or negative—always brings a benefit and a lesson.

The key to absolute trust lies in discerning what truly matters in your life and what doesn't, then acting in alignment with your choices. This isn't always easy. It can be confusing at times, but if you're willing to learn and keep going, your mind will clear, and you'll see with absolute clarity what's truly important.

2. Honesty

Honesty with yourself is simple: keep what you truly want and let go of what you don't. It sounds easy, but living this way requires deep trust in yourself and in Creation.

Great trust in yourself and Creation naturally sparks other qualities, like honesty. Being honest means being congruent—there's no contradiction between what you think, say, and do. Your entire being works in harmony.

THIS HARMONY CREATES A PEACEFUL, ABUNDANT LIFE WITH MINIMAL CONFLICT.

Conflict comes from self-deception. Someone who isn't congruent with themselves lives a life misaligned with their true self. In my experience, being completely honest in our thoughts, feelings, and actions is a challenge most of us face. It's one of humanity's most cherished values, yet it feels incredibly hard to achieve.

Our society has normalized lying as a tool for personal and professional goals. From childhood, we learn through family, school, and movies that a little white lie here and there is harmless.

Maybe one small lie doesn't seem to have a big impact at first. But what happens when that lie leads to another, and then another? You end up tangled in a confusing, conflict-filled world. Any resemblance to our current reality is, of course, pure coincidence.

Sometimes, we lie because we deliberately want to

deceive ourselves. Agreeing to do things you don't want to do—due to family, social, or fear-based pressures—only creates more anxiety and conflict.

Thanks to clinical research started in 1769 by William Cullen and continued in 1905 by Sigmund Freud, we know neurosis has a psychological origin. It stems from our struggles to cope with daily life's demands, moral conscience, and sexual or aggressive impulses.

Neurosis involves a range of psychological issues that show up as character traits, revealing unconscious desires and conflicts. When our minds hold contradictory desires, they manifest as anxiety, depression, or distress. Factors contributing to a neurotic personality include:

- Lack of affection
- Broken family dynamics
- Repressed desires
- Overprotection or neglect
- Traumatic childhood events (abandonment, abuse, loss of a parent or close relative, etc.)

These factors heavily influence a life of incongruence. Every day, we face events that test our level of congruence or incongruence.

This reminds me of a coaching client who sought help to overcome his excessive perfectionism. During sessions, he was impatient, expecting results from the very first meeting. He got frustrated with himself, calling himself "slow" or even "incapable" of making progress.

As we dug deeper into his life, I noticed he was highly perfectionist in specific areas but neglected others. At work, he obsessed over quick, perfect results. The fear of making mistakes or being reprimanded caused him intense anxiety.

Yet, in his personal life—like his self-care—he wasn't as demanding. He paid little attention to his diet or sleep schedule, with erratic rest patterns and no focus on healthy eating.

What struck me was that his perfectionism varied across different areas of his life. After our sessions, he had a breakthrough: he realized the areas causing him the most fear and anxiety were where he wasn't pursuing what he truly wanted.

At work, he aimed for perfection, but the job itself didn't excite him or align with his ideal career. Still, it offered responsibility, status, and corporate growth potential.

When he confronted this, he saw his obsession with perfection came from trying to meet external expectations and impress others, not from who he truly was. He confessed that, deep down, he longed for a simpler life, like running a small café.

This conflict between what he was doing and what he truly wanted created a void he tried to fill with perfectionist behaviors.

True honesty manifests as complete harmony between your thoughts, feelings, and actions. That congruence becomes an unshakable confidence in yourself.

3. Generosity

One of the biggest awakenings I've experienced is truly understanding what it means to give. In this world, giving often feels like losing something. If I give you a piece of my bread, I have less for myself.

For much of my life, I lived with this underlying fear of "losing." I struggled to trust others, afraid of a bad experience that might cost me time, money, confidence, or emotional well-being.

I used to think generosity was for saints, martyrs... or fools. Why give something if it means losing it? How wrong I was! Over time, as part of my own awakening, I realized giving and receiving are the same, as we've explored in earlier chapters.

As Rhonda Byrne says in *The Secret*, "The energy you give is the energy you receive." What you do for others, you do for yourself. Being generous in the fullest sense means living without fear, knowing that what you give is for yourself. It's part of the consciousness you create because you generate it.

Plant love, and you'll harvest love.
Plant fear, and you'll harvest fear.
Plant abundance, and you'll harvest abundance.
Plant scarcity, and you'll harvest scarcity.

The world works in a very practical, economical way. An apple tree can't grow pears. An elephant can't pretend to be a fish. The levels of being are clearly defined. What you project is what you are. If you achieve full trust in yourself, you'll experience the joy of living life as it truly is.

Let me share an example. When I worked at a large company, the culture was toxic—people rarely gave positive feedback. When things went well, no one said anything, but when things went wrong, complaints, accusations, and finger-pointing came fast.

It was a culture that drained performance and relationships. Tired of it, I decided to make a difference. I committed to thanking someone every day for their contribution and praising something I found valuable, without expecting anything in return.

At first, my colleagues were surprised. Some were skeptical, thinking I wanted something, but most accepted the compliments with gratitude. They said they didn't expect it, and some even told me my words brightened their day.

Over time, I noticed a transformation. My colleagues started giving me compliments, too. They were kinder and more willing to help. The team's dynamic became more positive, and the toxic atmosphere faded.

We turned a punitive, negative environment into one filled with good energy, trust, and respect. As a result, our team became one of the most efficient at delivering projects on time and successfully.

That was one of my first lessons in what it means to give generously. In this case, it was just words, but because they were sincere, they transformed an entire environment. The encouragement I gave came back to me multiplied.

I gained more than I imagined: colleagues who were a joy to work with, a harmonious workplace, and the trust of my bosses for delivering projects on time. No one lost—everyone improved!

Give with an open heart and complete trust that what you offer has value. What you give transforms the world. That, to me, is true generosity.

4. Patience

True love is cultivated through patience. Total love isn't in a hurry because it knows it contains everything. Impatience, in my view, is a form of fear or insecurity—like the fear that things won't turn out as you hope or the anxiety of getting a negative response. If you were certain that what you're waiting for will come positively and abundantly, you wouldn't feel impatient.

Someone who has a great relationship with their being knows the timing will be as perfect as the outcome. Patience comes naturally because they trust that God's timing is perfect.

You can't ask a flower to bloom faster than its natural process just because you're eager to see its colors or smell its fragrance.

You can't expect an oak tree to provide shade right away, either.

The majestic oak, with a lifespan of over 500 years, grows slowly, taking about 200 years to fully mature. If you want to enjoy its shade, you'll need to wait at least 15 years for it to start offering that blessing, which will expand year after year, long beyond a human lifetime. When you and I are gone, its shade will be more splendid than ever—a beautiful metaphor for patience!

In our modern world, being patient is increasingly difficult. The immediacy of daily life has conditioned us to expect quick, even instant, results. Immediacy is the enemy of patience. We can't cultivate healthy patience when we demand everything resolve as fast as possible.

I see patience as a dimension of love because it's a sign of total trust. It's a simple, elegant surrender to the present moment.

Developing genuine patience requires understanding what's truly valuable in the world and an inner wisdom aligned with the laws of Creation.

One of the biggest obstacles to patience is uncertainty. Many people struggle with this natural part of life. Uncertainty can paralyze us from chasing our dreams or making decisions that could bring great benefits, simply because we fear an uncertain future.

Someone with authentic, total patience sees life as timeless. They're completely certain that, in time, everything will work out, and there's no need to fear.

5. Open-Mindedness

The essence of love can only emerge from an open mind. Someone who truly loves can accept, understand, and embrace life without judgment. A closed mind blocks the truth, resists living fully, and shuts the door to enriching experiences, people, and feelings.

In a world divided by beliefs, ideologies, religions, and dogmas, opening your mind and listening with your heart is a true act of love. An open mind is one of the most visible acts of love toward Creation. Only those with an open mind can feel peace and see the world through eyes of love instead of resentment.

Let's pause for a moment to reflect on how you feel. Do you feel peace in your heart, or is something blocking it? Try this short exercise: Think of a person or situation you feel resentment toward (I suggest taking a couple of minutes with your eyes closed).

How do you feel thinking about that person or situation? You might notice discomfort—maybe a slight headache, a twinge in your foot, or an uneasy feeling in your stomach. These are repressed feelings stuck in your body, unable to find a way out.

You might find that thinking about that person brings up other situations where you felt wronged or mistreated. Your mind clouds over, replaying how badly they treated you, then recalling another distant event, and so on, until all you can see is how much they hurt you.

Now, once you've noticed that discomfort, repeat to

yourself: "Love holds no grievances. I will not betray my own being." Repeat it a few times. What effect does this phrase have on you?

Freeing your mind also frees the feelings tied to situations or people who, in our perception, "hurt us from the outside." We see everything as an external attack, where we're just victims.

Is opening your mind the same as opening your heart?

In my view, fully opening your mind requires an open heart. For example, you can't claim to be open to a new culture if, deep down, you criticize its way of life, customs, or traditions.

I've often seen people who move to a new country but never fully accept its culture. Instead of embracing it with an open heart, some reject it, criticize what they think is wrong, and cling even tighter to their culture of origin.

As someone who's lived in Switzerland for over 15 years, I've seen many foreigners who never adapt. Some, even after years in the country, keep complaining bitterly about everything: "The weather's awful," "The people are so closed-off," "They have no food culture," "They're racist," and so on.

Naturally, you wonder: *Why stay there, then?* It's a great question, and the answer—when you look at global migration—is complex and multifaceted. Common reasons include better job opportunities, education, financial prospects, or moving for a spouse or family member's homeland.

Whatever the reason, it shouldn't lead to feelings of separation or loss of identity. My point with this example is that an open mind means fully accepting life's nuances, even those we perceive as negative.

This doesn't mean an open mind lets you be attacked or manipulated. That's a key distinction—being open-minded isn't the same as accepting everything without question.

The human soul is sensitive and can easily fall victim to manipulation. As I've mentioned before, most of us have been shaped by both positive and negative influences.

When I talk about an open mind, I don't mean opening yourself to every manipulation or influence. Instead, it's about consciously choosing to see things as objectively as possible, accepting that much of human suffering comes from illusions created by our own minds.

We can choose to step out of that cloud of illusions and create our own reality. We can choose to love, live fully, and feel peace. It's a choice—your choice.

6. Faith

True faith, in my view, is fully understanding who you are and your purpose, accepting it without doubt or fear. To have unshakable faith in yourself requires absolute trust that every perceived obstacle has a solution.

It also demands honesty with yourself and seeing things clearly. It's committing 100% to your life's purpose, working tirelessly on yourself and your goals because you know they have value and meaning—they're your reason for being.

Faith is also about being generous with yourself, recognizing that the answers to all your problems lie within. It's forgiving yourself with an open heart for your mistakes.

Faith is having patience that everything will work out, trusting that the Creator's plans are meant to unfold perfectly. Faith doesn't waver—it's consistent and honest. It requires absolute trust in the powers of Creation. In my book *The Success Mindset*, I compare faith to the magical mechanism that turns a caterpillar into a butterfly.

We don't know exactly how faith works or what its mechanisms are. It's a power beyond rational explanation. Even Viktor Frankl, the Austrian neurologist, psychiatrist, and philosopher who survived Nazi concentration camps, found a fascinating link between those with deep faith and those without.

In his book *Man's Search for Meaning*, Frankl reflects: "Those who understand the close connection between a person's state of mind—their courage and hope, or lack thereof—and their immune system's capacity will see that a sudden loss of faith and hope can trigger a fatal outcome."*

---

* Frankl, Viktor. *Man's Search for Meaning*, Herder Editorial, p. 92 [Kindle version].

Like everything, every energy has its opposite. Some people develop fervent faith in the wrong things—like believing a spiritual or political leader will save them, that religion holds all the answers, or that the government will take care of them.

We must be honest with ourselves and develop the ability to channel faith in our favor. Everything comes from within, so we need to be careful about where we direct this superpower of faith.

My suggestion is to start with faith in yourself. Faith has a healing power, and we have a moral responsibility to heal ourselves first. Once you're healed, you can help heal your close family and, ultimately, society as a whole.

Chapter 9

Healing Your Relationship with Your Family

"The true root of all mental disorders is a lack of love in childhood. The only solution for mental disorders is love."
—Josep María Fericgla

The relationship with our parents is the first and most powerful influence we're exposed to from the moment we're born. The bond with our mother shapes our entire life. A loving, attentive, and happy mother creates a memorable, joyful, and warm childhood. An absent, neurotic, or depressed mother negatively impacts a child's environment, leading to growing up with anxiety, rebellion, and deep feelings of loneliness, among other struggles.

The relationship with our parents during childhood is, in my opinion, the most significant and impactful experience, with profound effects on how we navigate adulthood. Similarly, the relationship with our father and the experiences we have with him linger in our subconscious, shaping us in ways we sometimes feel we can't access or control.

If a child grows up with an alcoholic, abusive, or absent father, they're likely to unconsciously adopt some of those behaviors. According to Chilean artist, filmmaker, and writer Alejandro Jodorowsky, the family tree is a system of repetition that ensures the perpetuation of traditions, culture, heritage, and the preservation of the "clan's" legacy.

We enter this hierarchical system where belonging is crucial for family preservation. As a system for perpetuating the species, it's programmed into our subconscious. So, when we become aware of the clan and social groups, we develop a strong dependence on them. In other words, we do everything we can to feel accepted and to "belong" to our family.

Throughout my life, I've seen all kinds of cases where children end up studying a career or working in a profession just to "please their parents."

I vividly remember a friend from elementary school who took ballet classes after school. Back then, I loved spending sunny afternoons playing with friends, swimming, or simply savoring the freedom of summer evenings as a kid.

My friend didn't have that luxury. Every afternoon, she had to train for two to three hours at ballet. I'll never forget her sad look as she left school. One day, I asked if she wanted to come to my house to play after class. She replied:

—"I can't… I have to train for a ballet competition."

—"You must love those classes to go every afternoon without missing a single one," I said, with all the innocence of a child.

—"I actually hate ballet. I go because I have to. My mom wants me to be a professional ballerina—something she couldn't be when she had me."

Her response left me speechless, unsure of what to say. At the time, I didn't grasp the weight of her words. As a child, you don't have the maturity to reflect on life's complexities. But for some reason, that moment stuck with me, and to this day, I'm horrified by the kind of pressure parents put on their children.

OUR PARENTS, OFTEN UNCONSCIOUSLY, PROJECT THEIR SHORTCOMINGS, DREAMS, EXPECTATIONS, AND EVEN THEIR PERVERSIONS ONTO US.

As children, we often end up paying the price for our parents' broken dreams, fulfilling their unachieved aspirations as a kind of compensation for the "sacrifice" of bringing us into the world.

In his book *Timeless Inspirations*, Josep María Fericgla notes that the vast majority of psychological, emotional, and behavioral disorders people suffer from today have a common root: a lack of true love in childhood.

Alejandro Jodorowsky, in works like *The Dance of Reality* and *Psychomagic*, explains that his lack of connection with his parents drove him to explore film, art, and later psychoanalysis to find reconciliation with them, seeking to ease the deep loneliness and lack of love he experienced as a child.

Every illness stems from an unresolved conflict in childhood. Whether we were psychologically or physically mistreated or forced to do things we didn't want, it lodges in our deep consciousness and later surfaces as an illness or mental disorder.

Forgiving Your Parents Is the First Step to Healing

True healing starts at the root. A lack of love in childhood is one of the most significant and traumatic separations from unity for a human being. As Fericgla says, "Ten minutes of a parent's attention saves ten hours of therapy in adulthood."

If we want to heal our relationship with ourselves, we must start by forgiving our parents. This means raising our consciousness to a level where we can view emotional wounds objectively and with compassion.

Perhaps your parents weren't aware of the harm they caused, whether through neglect, ignorance, or carelessness. They might have been following the family clan's script, perpetuating—for better or worse—its patterns and traits.

The only remedy for healing is developing the ability to love yourself and others as an adult. Only when we awaken to the reality of true salvation can we dissolve the suffering that eats away at our soul for much of our life.

We've discussed forgiveness extensively in earlier chapters. True forgiveness, born from true love, is the only thing that can free us from the cave of illness and mental disorders.

Forgiving your parents is an act of love, but also an act of faith—a trust in life and Creation. It's recognizing that we are sacred, that our reality doesn't have to be shaped by buried emotions and feelings from the past that hold us back.

Forgive your mother with all your heart for the harm she caused unknowingly. Forgive your father for his absence or harsh treatment. I know it hurts. I know it's hard. Everything has a price, and forgiveness comes with its own.

You can choose not to forgive your parents, continuing the family clan's curse of pain, resentment, envy, and falsehoods. Or you can choose to forgive from the heart, freeing yourself from emotions that no longer belong to you and stepping into a reality where love has always been present, waiting to be recognized.

Perhaps the biggest mistake of our lives is not loving ourselves enough to keep suffering for the past. I know it's not easy, and sometimes it feels impossible without help. If needed, don't hesitate to seek support from a good professional. Your complete healing is at stake.

FORGIVING YOUR PARENTS IS THE GREATEST GIFT YOU CAN GIVE YOURSELF TO HEAL.

Heal Your Relationship with Your Siblings

Siblings are the second strongest social bond we're exposed to in childhood. Humanity's fundamental desire is to feel complete, protected, and loved.

When you have siblings, rivalry can emerge early on as you compete for your parents' full attention. As we saw earlier, most adults with depression are still dealing with mommy-daddy issues. They suffer from not being who they are, but who their family and society expect them to be—that's why there's this anguish to seek attention, craving the protection of fully present parents united by true love, treating them as unique.

Sadly, in our reality, that bond of true love between parents doesn't always form. As a result, the child accumulates emotional voids from physically and emotionally absent parents.

When a child faces the arrival of a sibling, the firstborn feels threatened; this new invader is stealing their spotlight with the parents. To protect the triad they're used to, the firstborn might treat the sibling with indifference, rivalry, or even violence to defend "their main spot."

I've seen this with my own siblings. As the oldest, I "enjoyed" all my parents' attention... until my brother was born. We played together, but there was a lot of rivalry. We fought for our parents' attention, especially Mom's. If he got more food or an extra toy, I'd get mad and feel "displaced."

I see it now with my own kids. My oldest daughter feels threatened whenever I give special attention to her little brother. If I serve breakfast and one notices the other got a bit more, a fight breaks out!

Studying the anxiety and conflicts between siblings over parental attention is the first step to gaining awareness and healing those old wounds.

Problems between siblings mainly stem from repeating the conflicts your father or mother had with their own siblings. As we've seen, the family tree is a pattern repeating the traits, stories, cultures, and pathologies of parents, grandparents, uncles, and even great-grandparents.

I know some siblings form strong friendships from childhood that flourish into adulthood, but sadly, that's not always the case. This intensifies feelings of loneliness and isolation.

With this in mind, you can consciously choose to foster a healthier relationship with your siblings: forgive them for childhood anxieties, understanding that something more beautiful than blood ties connects you. You're united by a shared love story, the potential for genuine and intense love, and the challenge of learning to share and enjoy things together.

Transcending the Family Tree

To truly heal, we must let the wounded child from our past become a mature adult, capable of taking the reins of their own destiny and creating their own reality.

Staying trapped in childhood creates the illusion that the family will miraculously change and all childhood conflicts will resolve "automatically." Many people wait their whole lives for their parents to acknowledge past mistakes and apologize.

Maturing means accepting the past with love and having the ability to leave it behind. If you keep holding onto old resentments, you don't make space for new relationships.

As we know, in this plane of existence, everything starts with the Self. It requires rigorous self-work to overcome and transcend the wounds left by the family tree. This involves facing buried subconscious emotions, bringing them to light, and examining them with adult awareness.

To do this, detach from the "family legend" to clarify events that marked your childhood, viewing them from "above," as a spectator, not a participant.

Then, make an effort to see things not as the wounded child—the victim who was attacked and mistreated—but as a calm witness observing without emotional involvement. This means facing past pains without fear.

Ultimately, detaching from the family tree's influences means transcending them and discovering your true nature: free, complete, and whole. Your family is an eternal source, not limited to the people you "inherited" at birth. After all, the family group is a tool for learning and discovering your true Self.

One of the biggest obstacles to transcendence is understanding that you don't have to sacrifice yourself to "save" the family. The family can only heal when each member freely and autonomously unfolds their talents and abilities.

In most cases, healing means becoming a new person—someone who recognizes themselves and can reinvent without carrying the family's emotional baggage.

Sacrificing your life for your parents (or another family member) doesn't heal the family; instead, it keeps them stuck in the cycle of unhealed wounds and unresolved issues.

Transcending the Fear of Failure

From my perspective, the fear of failure stems from the fear of "not being good enough" in your parents' eyes. By healing your relationship with them and freeing them from blame, you open the path to permanent healing that transcends the family and builds healthier societies—and ultimately, a healthier world.

According to Alejandro Jodorowsky in his book *Metagenealogía* (co-written with Marianne Costa), the fear of "not being" and "not belonging" boils down to six fundamental beliefs from a dysfunctional family relationship.

Recognizing and overcoming these beliefs is key to healing with your family.

First Belief: "I'm a bad person."

Feeling guilty for being born. Thinking things like "My family never accepted me for who I was," "My parents would have preferred I was born a boy (or girl)," maybe with different physical or intellectual traits—so you think "I'm a bad person" or "I couldn't live up to what was expected of me." The way to break free is to accept yourself as you are, from a place of love. You can't be anyone but yourself; you can only meet the expectations of being who you are.

Second Belief: "I don't have the right to leave my family."

Here, you believe you can't leave because of everything your parents have done for you. You feel responsible for caring for them. You fear something bad might happen if you abandon them. Some parents raise their kids not to be free and independent, but to stay and serve them in old age.

It's common for a manipulative mother to say to her children, "You're abandoning me now, after everything I've done for you, after sacrificing my career and life for you? Is this how you repay me?"

It's easy to fall into this subtle—or not-so-subtle—

manipulation. As a result, you feel guilty about "succeeding." You might sabotage opportunities like studying abroad or taking a job far away, fearing to leave your parents alone.

To reiterate, the only way to break free is to understand you came into the world for one mission: the complete and healthy realization of your Self.

Third Belief: "I don't have the right to feel pleasure. I don't have the right to be happy. I have to suffer to deserve it."

This belief is one of the deepest and hardest to heal, especially when you've been taught your whole life that you must earn a living and sacrifice because "life is suffering."

One of humanity's most sublime sources of happiness, in my opinion, is succeeding in your vocation and living off what you love. There's no purer pleasure than dedicating your life to what makes you truly happy. The peace of waking up each morning knowing you'll spend the day on your life's mission is incomparable.

Another great joy is enjoying the pleasure of being around only the people you truly love, even if it's just a few. Unfortunately, too many people think this vision of life is impossible—or only for the rich, privileged, or "kept" people who can afford the luxury of freedom over their time and work. Often, that belief comes from the family.

If your family tree has strong sexual repression, your

parents might have instilled that all pleasure is bad, from the devil, that too much happiness is "suspicious," and you're raised to doubt what makes you happy because "that's too good to be true" and life doesn't work that way —because "if you live off what you love, you'll starve"... unless you love being a real estate investor, politician, or company director.

Fourth Belief: "It's impossible to surpass my parents."

In one of my mentoring sessions, a client turning 40 shared her dream of becoming a professional ice skater. Her parents supported her skating lessons as a child.

According to her, "something weird" happened with her mom before competitions or big events. "My mom would get bad headaches, get really nervous, and we'd always arrive late to competitions," she said. So, she eventually packed away her dream of professional skating and prioritized college, studying Business Administration.

Digging into her past and family history, we uncovered an interesting story. Her mom was a professional ice skater but had to quit after an accident fractured her arm. That trauma was enough for her to abandon skating. Somehow, her frustration of not fulfilling her dream projected onto her daughter—so, perhaps unconsciously, she sabotaged her daughter's chance to surpass her in that field.

I can't say it happens in every case, but this is more

common than it seems. You'd think parents always want their kids to succeed, but in reality, even parents can suffer from Procuste Syndrome* with their children.

Of course, it's not just parents—it's common with siblings or close friends, too. I've also seen cases where it's not parents or friends sabotaging your success, but you self-sabotaging out of fear of "not fitting in" with the clan. For many, the pain of failure is more tolerable than being abandoned by family or friends.

Fifth Belief: "I'm a burden to my family."

When your parents remind you over and over that bringing you into the world was "a huge sacrifice." The family's incapacities and inconsistencies are loaded onto you. Maybe they remind you that "you were an accident," or that you caused financial problems.

There's always the mother who "sacrificed her career" to raise you.

Feeling like a burden to your family makes you believe you're a burden to society. You end up feeling unworthy of love, abundance, or full realization. In truth, your triumph is your family's triumph. Your happiness is a great contribution to the world.

---

* A term used to describe the attitude of those who try to hinder or minimize others' success out of fear of being left behind.

Sixth Belief: "I don't have the right to betray my family."

How many times have we held back from something we really wanted out of fear of "betraying" our parents?

A few years ago, I met a friend who adored his father. To him, his dad was his mentor and guide. My friend loved music and had an angelic voice. In his youth, he formed bands and performed at events as a hobby.

He was studying with me at the same university. Once, I asked if he'd seriously considered dedicating himself to music. He replied, "It'd be my dream, but my dad thinks singing is for lazy people and I'd never make a living that way. He wants me to be a great businessman, and that's what I'll do."

Years passed, and I lost touch except for what he posted on social media—until one day, he vanished completely. Unexpectedly, he reached out. We talked for a while, and he shared that his father had died prematurely and unexpectedly. "My dad was my mentor, my guide. Without him, I feel lost. I don't know what to do with my life now."

From his father's death, my friend began a painful process of reconnecting and healing with himself. He'd spent his life fulfilling his father's expectations to make him proud. With his dad gone, he faced an unrecognizable Self: himself. He tried to follow the path his father set, working as a corporate executive, until one day his consciousness betrayed him.

He fell into depression, and during a trip, he rediscovered himself. He reconnected with his inner voice, opening his eyes to his true destiny: music. He made perhaps the most important decision of his life—*to follow his inner voice*, his genie, and fulfill his mission. He left everything and now dedicates himself fully to music, which brings him immense happiness and satisfaction.

In my career as a mentor, I've witnessed many stories like this—hundreds of people giving up their Self out of fear of failure. And I don't mean financial failure. Sometimes it's not about money, but failing to meet the family mandate—usually from the father or mother, who often have the most influence in our lives.

Even I've been a victim of my family lineage. I studied Engineering just to be like my father, whom I deeply admired. When choosing my major, I didn't think if it passionate me or was my dream—I thought about how proud my dad would be seeing me graduate as an engineer like him, cheering me on from heaven.

Transcending the family tree becomes a true mission to reconnect with your inner genie. The inner genie is the God within you—infinite wisdom, sublime joy of living. It's creative, unifying, and *your true Self.*

Chapter 10

Healing Romantic Relationships

We could talk about romantic love enough to fill an entire book. As we've explored throughout this work, our relationships are like mirrors reflecting our level of consciousness.

Healing your romantic relationships depends on the initial healing you've done within yourself. Conflicts in relationships arise when you're trying to fill a void or meet an expectation your partner can't fulfill. In most cases, these expectations stem from past circumstances—painful childhood experiences or your relationship with your parents.

Over the years, I've often heard that a woman, for example, seeks in her partner the father she never had or wished for. And a man looks for the absent mother or one who didn't give enough affection.

So, if you do the initial inner healing—working hard on shifting your consciousness—it leads to making peace with your family tree. Once these two phases are addressed, romantic relationships often heal in the process.

The Key to True Love Lies in Detachment

Detachment is the key to healing in a romantic relationship. As psychologist Walter Riso says, detachment is "loving more and suffering less." Emotional dependence is one of the most common sources of conflict and suffering in relationships. This dependence can arise at any time for various reasons: low self-esteem, seeking security, compensating for a loss, needing success, sexual attachment, and so on. The important thing is to recognize what caused the dependence and why it feels so "addictive."

Emotional or sexual detachment can only happen when both partners recognize their personal freedom and autonomy. If there's a power struggle, with one partner feeling "dominated" (or actually being dominated), all sorts of conflicts and tensions will surface.

True love has nothing to do with dominating anyone. It's not about abandoning yourself to meet the other's needs or desires. It's not about being a servant or compensating for any family tree roles. Romantic love becomes authentic when both partners respect each other's independence and together seek to build a life project that helps them grow as human beings.

True Love: Building a Life Project Together

When two people unite in a mature, conscious, and selfless way, we can say they've reached the level of love known in Greek as *agápē*—a transcendent love that seeks the good of the beloved, where both work together to build something beyond their individual selfish desires.

For this kind of love to exist, personal healing must come first—meaning self-love, self-knowledge, and self-acceptance. A relationship at this level transcends even carnal or everyday desires, asking deeper questions: What's our ultimate purpose? What can transcend the love we feel for each other?

At this point, couples create a shared life project that contributes materially or spiritually to humanity—whether by starting a family, launching a business, pursuing education, creating art, or other endeavors.

Love stops being a *need* and becomes a *choice.* You consciously choose the steps you take together, no longer expecting the other to fix your flaws or creating false expectations. Fear of loss no longer paralyzes you, and fear stops driving the relationship.

Healing romantic relationships means taking responsibility for each other and building something truly valuable together. Your energies unite in a shared life project that transcends individuality. At this point, the energy of love opens the way to new, more transcendent levels of existence.

"My bounty is as boundless as the sea, my love as deep; the more I give to thee, the more I have, for both are infinite."

—William Shakespeare, *Romeo and Juliet* (Act II, Scene II)

Chapter 11

Healing Your Relationship with the World

"Self-acceptance is heroic because it means tearing down the internal limitations created by family, society, and culture."
—Alejandro Jodorowsky

You Never Meet Anyone by Chance

Every encounter we have throughout our life, even the smallest ones, serves a purpose of healing. When we pass someone on the street, it might not cross our mind that even the briefest meeting has a specific purpose, even if we're not aware of it.

Everything in the world has a defined purpose. I don't believe in coincidences. Every person who has crossed your path has taught you a lesson. We all support each other's evolution, whether we realize it or not.

That's why I'm convinced we should treat everyone we meet with respect and kindness, even those who act aggressively or unpleasantly. This doesn't mean letting anyone attack you. Being weak or passive isn't the same as projecting an inner strength so powerful that the influence of aggressors or mockers doesn't touch you.

If you're currently navigating a conflicted relationship —whether with a family member, friend, or colleague—ask yourself: *What lesson is this trying to teach me?* People are mirrors of our own shortcomings.

Think of someone you don't like. What about their personality bothers you? Maybe they're gossipy, impatient, or arrogant. Now, ask yourself: *In what ways are they like me? Do I recognize any of those traits in myself?*

I know self-criticism isn't easy. When we're in conflict with someone, it's simpler to blame them for the problem. We label them "intolerant," "rude," or "badly raised," casting ourselves as the poor victims of their mistreatment.

But when you look deeper, you realize that conflict seemingly coming from "outside" is actually a reflection of an inner lack manifesting through an unpleasant person or situation.

Once you understand this, you see that we create our own personal conflicts. When we observe violence, wars, or insensitivity in the world, we must ask ourselves how we're contributing to that collective reality.

How are we contributing to this collective image of a chaotic, violent, hopeless world? Why do we focus our attention on those aspects, knowing we have the power to choose?

Why choose to see a sick society lacking values and morality? Perhaps because we project our own shortcomings onto society. It's much easier to say "Society is sick" than "I am sick."

The first step to permanent healing, as I've mentioned throughout this book, starts with healing the *Self*. We can't give love or contribute positively to the world without first healing ourselves.

Expanding Your Consciousness

To progress, we need to set a goal that connects our inner world (our true identity) with the outer world (fulfilling our true destiny). This requires understanding how our consciousness interacts systematically with collective consciousnesses.

At the core is the Self—the consciousness that contains you as a person. The Self is central because it's where we perceive our individual consciousness. That consciousness is heavily shaped by family consciousness—the rules, traditions, and dynamics that mold your life from childhood to adulthood.

Family consciousness, in turn, is influenced by the collective consciousness of the society we live in. We adopt its language, customs, beliefs, and even religion. Society is shaped by the cultural consciousness of a specific region—like Western, Islamic, or Hindu culture.

Finally, we reach the collective human consciousness. We know we all belong to planet Earth, that we're all *Homo sapiens*, sharing the same sky, sun, water, and land.

When we say we want to live in a healthy, happy world, what we're really desiring is a healthy, happy life for ourselves. There's no other way to achieve this than by starting with yourself.

When you heal, you can forgive the restrictive forces of your family. You see your parents with eyes of love and compassion, transcending the illusory prison of those beliefs. You realize you don't have to "make your parents proud" or owe your grandparents anything. You don't have to sacrifice your life to perpetuate restrictive forces!

By overcoming that barrier, you also see that you don't owe society anything. You don't have to perpetuate the conflict between being and belonging. You're not obligated to follow norms, religions, traditions, or taboos.

With your liberation, you open the door to the energy of unity with the world.

Ultimately, fulfilling your personal project helps unify the world. The world benefits when your creative future is realized. The small Self, starting from that tiny core, becomes an expansive energy that transforms the world.

The universal law of Creation is the law of expansion. All consciousness must expand and grow because that's our role in the world. It's no different from the role of plants, animals, or any conscious being. The opposite of expansion is repression. As unique, creative beings, it's our duty to act consciously, always expansively, seeking unity.

Liberating Your genie Is Expanding Your Consciousness

At the end of the journey, we know that truly liberating our inner genie is a lifelong struggle. Freeing yourself from the carefully crafted ego; from repressive energies like family tree stories, personal and emotional ties; from fears, lacks, emotional and sexual dissatisfaction, and useless needs instilled by modern consumerism—all of this demands a constant fight against the image you've created of yourself in the world.

The more that light of consciousness awakens in you, the more your vital, creative energy is freed. You awaken to a reality where miracles truly happen. By "miracles," I don't mean spectacular events like making a car appear out of nowhere, raising the dead, or levitating in front of a crowd. I mean the true miracles: the full recognition that life itself is the miracle.

The miracle of your heartbeat. The miracle of every breath. The miracle of feeling, at every moment, the vital force called life working tirelessly to offer you this experience.

The miracle happens when we join the creative force, when we let it carry us. When we humbly offer our Self to the vastness, contributing our small (but essential) part to unity.

The miracle is seeing life with a new consciousness, through which we lose the fear of being who we are. We dare to *Be*. As Alejandro Jodorowsky says, "Birds fly without fear of crashing into the wind."

Immortality

Those who know others are intelligent;
those who understand themselves are
enlightened.
Those who conquer others have strength;
those who master themselves are
powerful.
Those who dare to face death have
courage;
but those who cannot be destroyed by it
are immortal.
—*Lao Tzu,* Tao Te Ching

Appendix

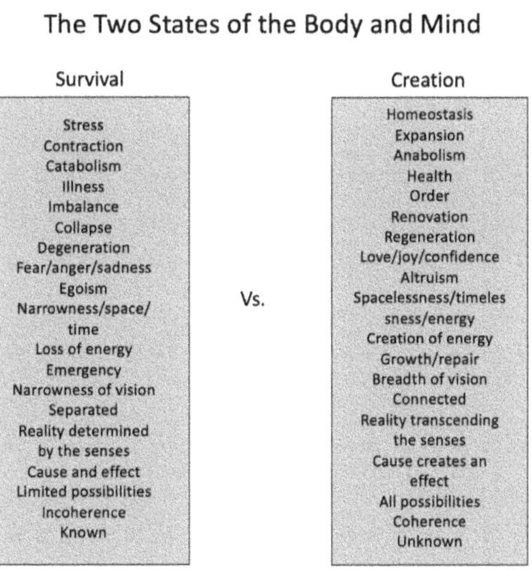

Figure 1: The "Survival State" versus the "Creation State."

Source: Dispenza, Joe. Breaking the Habit of Being Yourself, Editorial Urano, p. 148 [Kindle version].

I'd Love Your Feedback

I'd love to hear what you think of *Awaken Your Inner Genie*. Your feedback is an invaluable gift to me, helping me refine my message so I can offer you the best of myself in future publications.

You can write a review on the platform where you got the book or send me a personal message at info@paolaknecht.com. I also invite you to follow me on social media:

- Instagram: @paolaknecht_author
- X: @PaolaKnecht
- LinkedIn: www.linkedin.com/in/paolaknecht/

About the Author

Paola Knecht is an author, mindset and transformation coach, and therapist in clinical training, committed to personal development and holistic well-being. With five books published in Spanish and English — including The Success Mindset and The Secrets of Discipline — her writing has accompanied readers around the world on the path toward a more conscious and fulfilling life.

With over fifteen years of experience in engineering and strategic management at globally recognized companies, Paola chose to redirect her expertise toward what truly moves her: understanding the human mind and accompanying people in their transformation. Today she combines her coaching practice with advanced studies in clinical psychology and psychotherapy, deepening her understanding of the scientific and therapeutic side of change.

She lives in Switzerland with her husband and children, and works with an international audience.

To follow her publications and learn more about her work, visit: paolaknecht.com

Coaching and accompaniment at savia.paolaknecht.com

Monthly reflections at paolaknecht.com/newsletter

instagram.com/paolaknecht_author

tiktok.com/@paolaknecht29

Bibliography

Abundancia, R. (2025) «Poco sexo y más amistad: ¿qué idea del amor tienen las nuevas generaciones?». El País. https://elpais.com/estilo-de-vida/2025-02-14/poco-sexo-y-mas-amistad-que-idea-del-amor-tienen-las-nuevas-generaciones.html, acceso 31 de marzo 2025.

Álvarez, A. (2014) «La ética en las -nanzas islámicas». Revista de la Universidad Internacional de La Rioja. https://dialnet.unirioja.es/descarga/articulo/4901220.pdf, acceso 10 de marzo 2025.

Batlle Caminal, J. (2019) «El teléfono tiene la culpa de que tengas menos sexo». ABC Tecnología. https://www.abc.es/tecnologia/abci-telefono-tiene-culpa-tengas-menos-sexo201905082332_noticia.html, acceso 31 de marzo 2025.

Bernard, R. (2018) «Revelations by an insider» [Video en YouTube]. https://www.youtube.com/watch?v=uLNvpogVzzk, acceso 16 de marzo 2025.

BBC Mundo (2023) «Niksen: La solución holandesa para reducir el estrés».https://www.bbc.com/mundo/vert-tra-65683334, acceso 9 de enero 2025.

Biblia Latinoamericana (1997) La Biblia Latinoamericana, Editorial Clie.Boseley, S. (2019) «Britons having less sex and digital life may be to blame -study». The Guardian. https://www.theguardian.com/lifeandstyle/2019/may/07/britain-sex-decline-study-married-cohabiting-couples-digital-life, acceso 13 de febrero 2025.

Byrne, R. (2006) El secreto, Editorial Urano.

Carmona, R. (2021) «¿Te cuesta parar? Practica el niksen, el arte holandés de no hacer nada». La Vanguardia, https://www.lavanguardia.com/vivo/lifestyle/20210307/6262802/niksen-arte-holandes-no-hacer-nada.html, accessed 9 de enero 2025.

Casillas Estrella, M.; Montaño Castrejón, N.; Bacardí Gascón, M. & Jiménez Cruz, A. (2007) «Mexicanas con mayor insatisfacción de laimagen corporal». Atención Primaria, 39(2), p. 105. https://www.

elsevier.es/es-revista-atencion-primaria-27-articulo-mexicanas-con-mayor-insatisfaccion-imagen-13098680?utm_, acceso 13 de febrero 2025.

Castro, C. (2025) «La cifra millonaria que gana Bonnie Blue en Only-Fans, la joven que se acostó con 1000 hombres en 12 horas». Infobae. https://www.infobae.com/entretenimiento/2025/04/14/la-cifra-millonaria-que-gana-bonnie-blue-en-onlyfans-la-joven-que-se-acosto-con-1000-hombres-en-12-horas/, acceso 18 de abril 2025.

Centro Budista de la Ciudad de México. (s. f.) «Budismo, Mindfulness154 Bibliografía y Dinero». https://budismo.org.mx/material/estudio/articulos-budismo/08-budismo-mindfulness-y-dinero.pdf, acceso 10 de marzo 2025.

Coleman, R. (1992) John Lennon: The de!nitive biography, Heinemann.

Curie, M. (s. f.) Pierre Curie. Classic Literature Library. https://classic-literature.net/marie-curie-1867-1934/pierre-curie/, acceso 20 de abril 2024.

Dweck, C. S. (2006) Mindset: The new psychology of success, Random House.

Duno, M. & Acosta, E. (2019) Percepción de la imagen corporal en adolescentes universitarios. Revista chilena de nutrición, 46(5), pp. 545-553. https://dx.doi.org/10.4067/S0717-75182019000500545, acceso 13 de febrero 2025.

Elefante. (s. f.) «Durmiendo con la luna» [Letra de canción], https://www.letras.com/elefante/12434/, acceso 10 de octubre 2024.

EduKitchen (2024) Chomsky on ChatGPT, Education, Russia and the unvaccinated [Video en YouTube], https://www.youtube.com/watch?v=IgxzcOugvEI

Fericgla, J. M. (2022) Inspiraciones sin tiempo: Máximas de un antropólogo para alentar el futuro de nuestros hijos, Barcelona, Editorial Escola de Vida.

Fuzeiro, V.; Martins, C.; Gonçalves, C.; Santos, A. R. & Costa, R. M. (2022) «Sexual function and problematic use of smartphones and socialnetworking sites». The Journal of Sexual Medicine, 19(8), pp. 1303-1308.https://doi.org/10.1016/j.jsxm.2022.05.004, acceso 23 de marzo 2025.

Frankl, V. E. (1991) El hombre en busca de sentido. Barcelona, Editorial Herder.

Freud, S. (2001) The complete psychological works of Sigmund Freud: «An infantile neurosis» and other works (Vol. 17). Vintage.

Greene, R. (2018) The Laws of human nature, Penguin Random House.

Grinberg-Zylberbaum, J. (1994) El Yo como idea. México: Instituto Nacional para el Estudio de la Conciencia (INPEC).

Hawkins, D. R. (s. f.) El poder frente a la fuerza: Los determinantes ocultos del comportamiento humano, Editorial El grano de mostaza, p. 74 [versiónKindle].

Hill, N. (2015) Piense y hágase rico (Edición Diamante), Estados Unidos, Aimee SBP.

Housel, M. (2020) The psychology of money: Timeless lessons on wealth, greed, and happiness, Harriman House.

Isaacson, W. (2011) Steve Jobs, Simon & Schuster.

Jodorowsky, Alejandro & Costa, Marianne (2009) Metagenealogía: El árbol genealógico como arte, terapia y búsqueda del Yo esencial, Barcelona, Penguin Random House.

Jodorowsky, A. (2001) La danza de la realidad, Barcelona, Editorial RBA.

Jodorowsky, A. (1995) Psicomagia: La terapia del alma, Editorial Atalanta.

Kaizen Institute (s. f.) Domina los Fundamentos de KAIZEN™ Lean, https://kaizen.com/es/insights-es/domina-fundamentos-kaizen/, acceso 5 de marzo 2025.

Knoff, W. F. (1970) «A history of the concept of neurosis, with a memoir of William Cullen». American Journal of Psychiatry, 127(1), pp. 80-84. https://doi.org/10.1176/ajp.127.1.80, acceso 24 de marzo 2025.

La Rochefoucauld, F. (1867) Ré!exions, sentences et maximes morales de La Rochefoucauld (C. A. Sainte-Beuve, L. D. C. Vauvenargues & J. B. A. Suard, Eds.), Garnier Frères, https://www.loc.gov/item/tmp96031343/, acceso 12 de noviembre 2024.

Lao Tzu (2021) Tao Te Ching: The Book of the Way (Sam Todore Book Arts, Ed.), Sam Todore Book Arts.

Levy, B. R.; Slade, M. D.; Kunkel, S. R. & Kasl, S. V. (2002) «Longevity increased by positive self-perceptions of aging». Journal of Personality and Social Psychology, 83(2), pp. 261-270.

MedlinePlus (s. f.) Trastorno por dé1cit de atención con hiperactividad (TDAH). Biblioteca Nacional de Medicina de EE.UU. https://medlineplus.gov/spanish/attentionde1cithyperactivitydisorder.html, acceso 10 de octubre 2024.

Newport, C. (2012) So Good they can't Ignore You: Why Skills Trump Passion in the Quest for Work You Love, New York, Business Plus.

Real Academia Española (2024) En Diccionario de la lengua española (versión 23.8). https://dle.rae.es/, acceso 10 de octubre 2024.

Ramos Agrela, M. (2024) Somatización: cuando el cuerpo expresa lo que la mente calla. Top Doctors, https://www.topdoctors.es/articulos-medicos/somatizacion-cuando-el-cuerpo-expresa-lo-que-la-mente-calla/, acceso 17 de febrero 2025.

Ratzinger, J. (2023) Vivir como si Dios existiera: una propuesta para Europa, R. Calleja Editor/Ediciones Encuentro.

Reich, W. (s. f.) The bioelectrical investigation of sexuality and anxiety, WRM Press [versión Kindle].

Reich, W. (1953) The murder of Christ: The emotional plague of mankind, Farrar, Straus and Giroux.

Riso, W. (2007) Manual para no morir de amor, Barcelona, Editorial Océano.

Sánchez, G. (2012) Sabios de Sión: Los Protocolos (Edición en español), CreateSpace Independent Publishing Platform.

Schucman, H. (2018) Un Curso de Milagros (R. M. Wynn & F. Gómez, trads.), Foundation for Inner Peace.

Shakespeare, W. (1597) Romeo y Julieta (Acto III), Project Gutenberg, https://www.gutenberg.org/ebooks/1112, acceso 9 de abril 2025.

Srnicek, N. (2018) Capitalismo de plataformas, Buenos Aires, Editorial Caja Negra.

Tallero, T. (1996) El cuerpo como delito: anorexia, bulimia, cultura y sociedad, Barcelona, Editorial Ariel.

Vallespinós, E. (2024) «Te veo más delgada». El País. https://elpais.com/opinion/2024-08-18/te-veo-mas-delgada.html, acceso 13 de febrero 2025.

Ytturralde, E. (2023) El Síndrome de Procusto. https://yturralde.com/articulo-sindrome-de-procusto.html, acceso 4 de abril 2025.

Wilson, T. D. (2002) Strangers to ourselves: Discovering the adaptive unconscious, Cambridge, MA: Belknap Press of Harvard University Press.

Take back the leadership of your mind
The Success
MINDSET
Paola Knecht

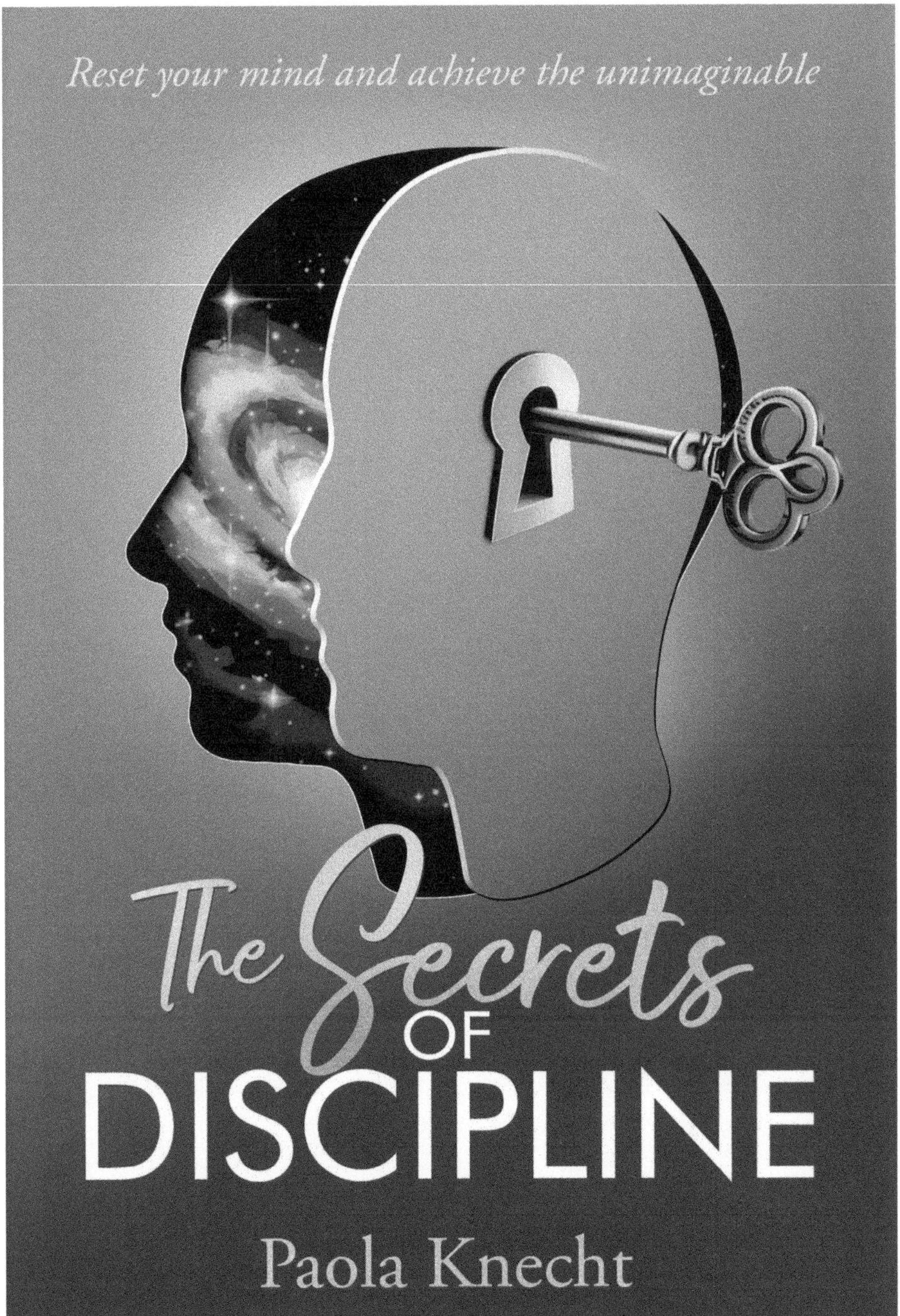

Reset your mind and achieve the unimaginable
The Secrets
OF
DISCIPLINE
Paola Knecht

A World of Illusions
A Wake-Up Call
and the Search for the Truth
PAOLA KNECHT

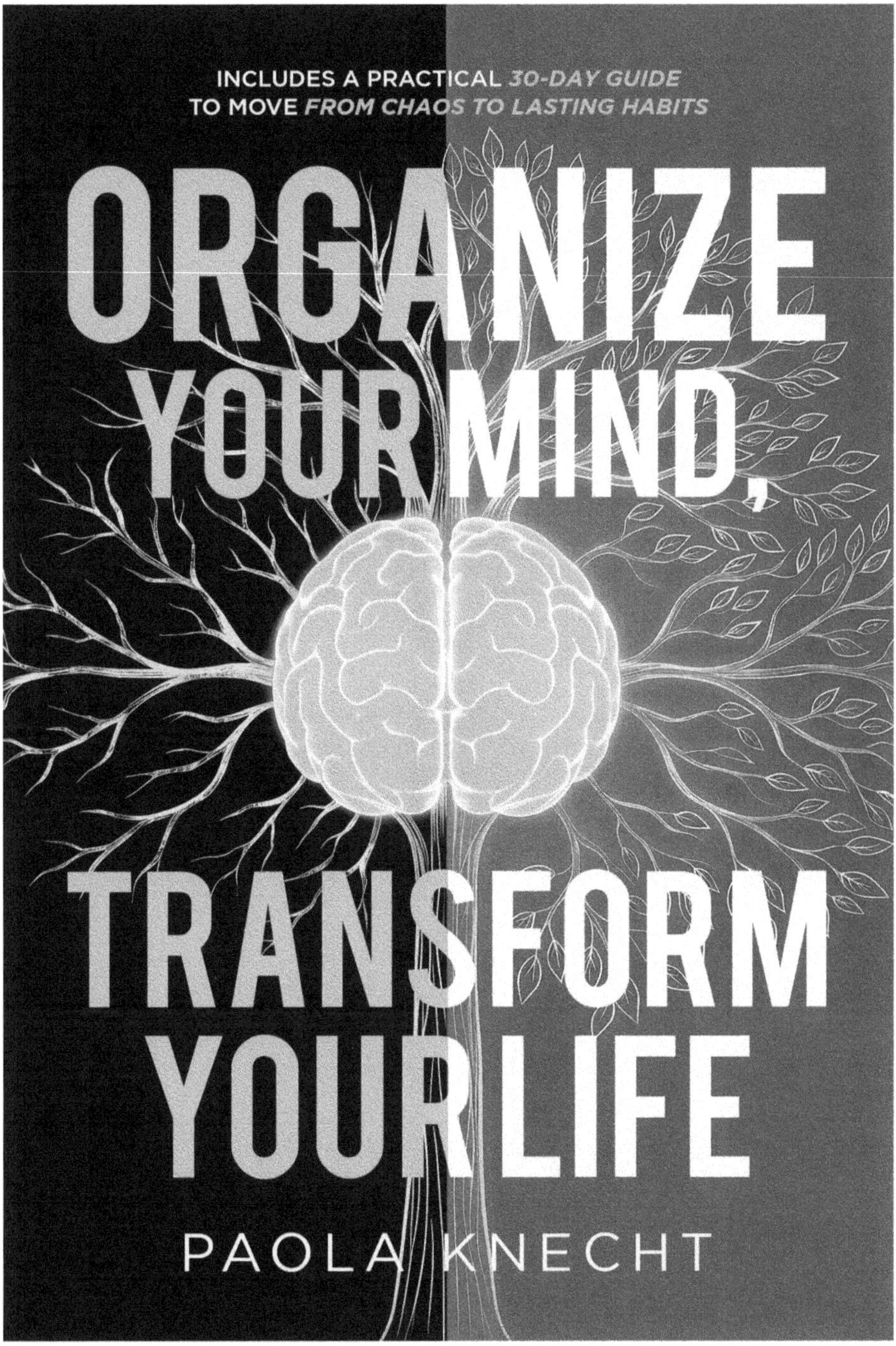
INCLUDES A PRACTICAL 30-DAY GUIDE
TO MOVE FROM CHAOS TO LASTING HABITS
ORGANIZE YOUR MIND,
TRANSFORM YOUR LIFE
PAOLA KNECHT

www.ingramcontent.com/pod-product-compliance
Lightning Source LLC
Chambersburg PA
CBHW041259210926
51847CB00009B/75
9783952628348